RED CHINA

MAO CRUSHES CHIANG'S KUOMINTANG, 1949

D1344435

GERRY VAN TONDER

Pen & Sword
MILITARY

To my wife Tracey

First published in Great Britain in 2018 by
PEN AND SWORD MILITARY
an imprint of
Pen and Sword Books Ltd
47 Church Street
Barnsley
South Yorkshire S70 2AS

The author gratefully acknowledges key source material obtained from declassified
Central Intelligence Agency documents and the British Newspaper Archive.
Special thanks to Miguel Miranda for his preliminary research

ISBN 978 1 52670 810 6

Typeset by Aura Technology and Software Services, India
Printed and bound by CPI Group (UK) Ltd, Croydon, CR0 4YY

Pen & Sword Books Ltd incorporates the imprints of Pen & Sword
Archaeology, Atlas, Aviation, Battleground, Discovery, Family History, History, Maritime, Military,
Naval, Politics, Railways, Select, Social History, Transport, True Crime, Claymore Press, Frontline
Books, Leo Cooper, Praetorian Press, Remember When, Seaforth Publishing and Wharncliffe.

For a complete list of Pen and Sword titles please contact
Pen and Sword Books Limited
47 Church Street, Barnsley, South Yorkshire, S70 2AS, England
email: enquiries@pen-and-sword.co.uk
website: www.pen-and-sword.co.uk

CONTENTS

The Manchurian or Pneumonic Plague broke out when the imperial court in Beijing was at its weakest just prior to Sun Yat-sen's revolution. With a near 100% mortality rate, its outbreak would claim the lives of 45,000 to 60,000 Harbin residents. This photo has erroneously been ascribed to Japanese atrocities in Manchuria. (Photo Spike Cook via Thomas H. Hahn)

The Rape of Nanking or 'Viol de Nankin': a graphic mural. (Photo by Thierry Ehrmann)

TIMELINE

1911

10 October: Beginning of the 1911 Revolution; the Qing Dynasty is overthrown.

1919

4 May: Students and anarchists launch the May Fourth Movement to protest Japan's annexation of Chinese territory.

1921

12 July: Founding of the Chinese Communist Party (CCP) in Shanghai.

1925

12 March: Sun Yat-sen dies from cancer.

1927

27 August: The Nanchang Uprising begins and is defeated the following month.
7 September: The Autumn Harvest Uprising begins in Hunan and is also a failure.
October: Founding of Jiangxi–Fujian Chinese Soviet.
December: Chiang Kai-shek returns to China, becoming generalissimo.

1933

25 September: Chiang Kai-shek launches the Fifth Extermination campaign.

1934

10 October: Start of the Long March. The Jiangxi–Fujian Soviet is evacuated.

1935

19 October: The First Front Army arrives in Shanxi; the Long March ends.

1936

12–25 December: Xi'an Incident takes place, a political crisis culminating in the seizure of the Nationalist generalissimo Chiang Kai-shek by two of his own generals, Zhang Xueliang and Yang Hucheng.

1937

7 July: The Marco Polo Bridge incident triggers the Second Sino-Japanese War.

13 August: Battle of Shanghai.

13 December: Nanking falls to the Japanese.

1941

7 January: The CCP's New Fourth Army clashes with Kuomintang (KMT) units.

7 December: The Japanese attack Pearl Harbor.

1944

17 April: Operation Ichi-go commences.

1945

9 August: The Soviet Red Army invades Manchuria.

15 August: Japan surrenders.

29 August: Mao Zedong flies to Chungking to negotiate a coalition government with the KMT; Communist Chinese forces begin entering Manchuria.

1946

23 May: Partial withdrawal of Soviet Red Army from Manchuria.

July: Founding of People's Liberation Army (PLA); civil war resumes.

1948

27 August: Beginning of the Huai-Hai campaign.

October: PLA strength reaches 1.8 million.

23 November: The Huai-Hai campaign ends, during which the KMT loses 400,000 men.

1949

January: The KMT garrison in Peking surrenders.

10 October: The Communist Chinese hold a victory parade in Peking; Mao Zedong announces the creation of the People's Republic of China (PRC).

INTRODUCTION

The epic proportions of the tragedy of the country that is China before, during and after the Second World War, is difficult to perceive in terms of sheer magnitude and scale. The cold statistic of 13 million casualties sustained during the war offers a semblance of the problems that confronted the nation's ideologically diverse leaders after Japan's capitulation.

Initially, the prominent role played by the Nationalists during the conflict seemed set to take China through the healing process and into a complicated future. However, such appearances were deceiving. Mao Zedong's brand of people-centred communism ensured his hold over vast areas of northern China, while Chiang Kai-shek's nationalist regime appeared bent on self-destruction as a miscellany of failures frustrated even his most loyal allies.

The closing stages of the Second World War in Asia was a Soviet affair. With Berlin captured by the victorious Red Army, ending the war in Europe, the wily Joseph Stalin redirected his military resources towards the Far East. In the northeastern Chinese puppet state of Manchukuo—'State of Manchuria'—acquired by Japan in 1931, a vast agro-industrial empire had grown in isolation as the war in the Pacific effectively kept the region out of the war. The Kwantung Army, an army group of the Imperial Japanese Army, governed Manchukuo, its chiefs of staff holding the top military and civil administration positions. Originally formed as a garrison to protect the railroads paid for by Japanese banks, over a period of twenty-five years the Kwantung Army outgrew its humble beginnings, peaking at a strength of more than 1.3 million, assuming an exaggerated importance.

Its officers were complicit in the Mukden Incident in 1931 that implicated China, thereby justifying the seizure of the territory. Its role in the Marco Polo Bridge incident in 1937 launched the bitter Sino-Japanese War.

But for much of the Great Pacific War, as Tokyo called its struggle with the Allies from 1941 until 1945, the Kwantung Army remained idle, having little use in any theatre. As a result, it had grown large, impressive, and impotent.

On 9 August 1945, just three days after 'Little Boy' incinerated Hiroshima and coinciding with the same terrible hours when a flight of B-29s delivered 'Fat Man' to Nagasaki, the Soviet Red Army sealed Manchukuo's fate. Slicing across Outer

Mongolia on horseback, muleback, on foot and truck and tread, one half of a giant pincer carved a path to encircle the Kwantung Army in China's dusty central plains.

The other pincer, ferried by river boats across the Amur and Usuri rivers, barrelled down on the Japanese with violent force, their path softened by the largest Soviet airborne operation of the war. Like the rest of Imperial Japan's legions, the Kwantung Army was full of ardent soldiers equipped with inadequate weapons. Armoured cars and light tanks were the best that could be mustered against the Soviet T-34s. From radios to howitzers, Japan's soldiers were ill-prepared to face off against the combined arms of their nemesis.

The remnants of the Kwantung Army surrendered en masse a week before the United States hailed VJ Day. The spoils of Manchukuo were for the Soviets to do with as they pleased. This meant the wholesale appropriation—more like pillaging—of machine tools, generators, raw materials, and whatever else could be disassembled and sent back to the Russian heartland. Included among this booty were unwanted Japanese prisoners numbering hundreds of thousands, well-appointed administrative buildings of a government that no longer existed, and the former Chinese Emperor Pu Yi, who was once again exiled—this time to the Soviet Union.

Emperor Puyi wearing Manchukuo uniform.

The New Emperor of Manchukuo

Pu Yi Enthroned

Hsingking, Manchuria

With quaint religious rites recalling China of the past, Pu Yi, the ex-boy Emperor of China, this morning became Emperor of the Japanese-protected realm of Manchukuo and its 30,000,000 inhabitants, under the title of Kang Teh ("tranquillity and virtue").

This was the second time Pu Yi had been made emperor, for at three years of age he ascended the throne of the Chinese Empire under the name of Hsuau Tung. But his father, Prince Chun, then ruled in his name until the revolution swept away the regime.

To-day's ceremonies were divided into two parts—the religious observances dating back many centuries and the enthronement.

The first took place near the site of the future palace. In a square enclosure, screened by bunting of Imperial yellow, to a height of 12 feet, a circular "Altar of Heaven," seven feet high and 27 feet across, had been erected.

In the chill but clear air of the early morning, the highest officials of the new Manchu Empire had taken up their allotted positions. The distant strains of band music heralded the approach of the Emperor, through heavily guarded streets. He drove in a bullet-proof motor car, convoyed by nine other cars, containing his armed guard, and flanked by six motor cycles, with sidecars, filled with picked police.

As Pu Yi emerged from his car, he was seen to be wearing a fur-trimmed, pearl-bedecked hat, with red tassels, and a blue gown, richly embroidered with golden dragons and other symbols, the sleeves being of dark red. His outer coat, emblazoned with the Imperial dragon, bore the inscription in ancient characters: "Jih yueh wan shou"—"Ageless like the sun and moon."

The ceremony over, the Imperial party sped swiftly back through the silent streets to the palace. Troops kept citizens at a safe distance from the Emperor's route.

Belfast News-Letter,
Friday, 2 March 1934

But while the Soviet investment of Manchuria, its proper westernized name, seemed like a timely effort that hastened the war's end, it did give Moscow a perfect opportunity to return favours; though not to the Americans, whose merchant fleet had delivered millions of tons in lend-lease aid over the past five years. China's government, the Kuomintang (KMT), being so reliant on American support, allowed 50,000 marines to deploy in Manchuria to help the Soviets disarm and repatriate the resident Japanese population. But an attempt at delivering US marines to the old imperial capital of Peiping (also Beiping, later Peking / Beijing), and Qingdao was refused. The Soviets were just as steadfast in holding on to Port Arthur in the Liaotung Peninsula jutting along the rim of the Yellow Sea. As a further affront, the KMT was blocked from reclaiming Manchurian cities, which flew in the face of the Chiang Kai-shek regime's Treaty of Friendship with the Soviet Union.

Hidden in the minutiae of Soviet archives, the gambit playing out in Manchuria was the crowning glory for an audacious attempt to spread Moscow's influence. Since 1919, agents of the nascent Soviet Union were laying the groundwork for the twentieth century's most daring geopolitical project—bringing communism to Asia. Often resulting in minor gains at the cost of enormous losses, in 1945 the Red Army became a willing accomplice to the astute Mao Zedong and his People's Liberation Army (PLA), who had spent the last ten years encircled in a remote corner of Shanxi, their final redoubt after the dreadful Long March.

Warlord Yan Xishan's soldiers, Zuoquan County, Shanxi Province, 1925.

In a matter of months, some 300,000 troops, under the veteran PLA commander Lin Biao, crossed over to Manchuria. Experts at manoeuvre and subterfuge, the newly formed corps was allowed to equip themselves with captured Japanese weapons, and even received training at Kiamusze, a semi-clandestine staging ground near the Sino-Soviet border.

Years before the KMT had imposed a 'United Front' on the communists, who were surrounded by nearly half a million National Revolutionary Army (NRA) troops—Chiang's armed forces—in their mountain enclave. The communists did pitch in, conducting a broad guerrilla campaign against Japanese-controlled cities and bases, although most of the time they were fighting Chinese 'turncoat' forces conscripted for garrison duty. In 1941, however, the CCP's New Fourth Army clashed with KMT regular divisions, proving that the United Front bonds were far from permanent.

But Mao and his generals knew how to bide their time. In August 1945, Mao was flown to the capital Chungking for a conference with Chiang and the KMT leadership. The end of the war against Japan allowed the Allies to take stock. In the Chinese theatre, anywhere between 20 and 30 million civilians had died in the cruel years between 1937 and 1945. Since China had fought so desperately against the odds, she had lost a further 3.5 million soldiers. It was estimated that a quarter of China's population was internally displaced or had lost their homes. The government was bankrupt and local industries were either destroyed or had been looted. Perhaps, as the Americans suggested, it was time to establish a lasting peace?

Mao was in Chungking until 10 October. He would participate in another round of talks in January the following year, this time with US General George C. Marshall doing his best to broker a power-sharing agreement between the factions.

Unknown to the Americans, the Chinese Communists had spent months preparing for all-out war against the KMT. What in previous years had been a genuine peasant army that travelled by foot was, in the space of less than a year, flush with rifles and machine guns, tanks and artillery, and with a total strength of 1.3 million.

By 1947, the hopes for a permanent United Front had disappeared without a trace. With much of north and northeast China reeling from the just-concluded world war, both sides readied themselves for a final struggle. The stakes could not have been higher. Whatever China could aspire to become, as a unified country commanding the largest population on earth, it had first to choose a course. Mao's communists wanted perpetual revolution to replace the vestiges of the dynastic past. Chiang and the KMT, on the other hand, sought a place among the nations of the world.

1. THE REVOLUTION

The Chinese Communist Party (CCP) was born at a clandestine meeting overseen by a foreign agent. For years prior, lone provocateurs of the Communist International, or Comintern, stalked China's cities and sought out local ideologues. Liberal ideas had spread across the mainland since before the turn of the century. Sun Yat-sen's successful revolt in 1911 was supposed to be the shattering climax of this process, being the singular force that caused the weakening Qing Dynasty downfall. Sun and his allies expected to usher a new era of modernity that would launch China onto the world stage. Or so it was hoped. Sun's ambitions were quickly thwarted by Yuan Shikai, a veteran Qing commander who turned on the empire and assumed the role of dictator. Sun went into bitter exile as a result and southern China was torn apart by warlords for several years. Unable to impose a semblance of national unity, the ageing Yuan died in 1916 and left the Republic of China in tatters.

In this ferment far greater, destructive Western ideas took hold. With the nation gripped by a convoluted civil war from 1912 until 1920, the social bonds it frayed led to a newfound nationalism, seething with outrage that viewed China as a powerless hostage to foreign aggression. In 1919, the short-lived May Fourth Movement, with its widespread protests against Japanese violations of Chinese sovereignty, breathed life into the wildest dreams of intellectual dilettantes.

While the Christian faith had established a firm foothold in China, thanks to the tireless efforts of missionaries and teachers, the same zeal and devotion compelled local firebrands to proselytize the virtues of socialism and anarchism wherever these ideas found converts. Socialism already appealed to China's millions of downtrodden peasants, who eked out a meagre living from estates controlled by landlords. The violence of anarchism, with its attractive belligerence toward authority in a culture obsessed with deference toward one's betters, nurtured its own misfits, and it was far more likely to find anarchist gangs plotting in China's larger cities than local cadres of Bolsheviks.

Indeed, for the young Mao Zedong—born in a village idyll in 1893—the siren call of revolution came to him gradually. Although he had enlisted as a teenage soldier in a warlord's army during the initial disturbances following the 1911 revolt, which was launched in southern China and then spread north, he had little

The Chinese Rebellion

New York, Saturday—The "New York American" states that Sun-Yat-Sen, who is living at Denver, Colorado, has left that city, and is now en route for New York.

Foreign Ships at Hankow
There is no change in the situation here. Four British, two German, two American, and two Japanese warships are protecting the foreign concessions, and two Chinese cruisers, two gunboats, and four torpedo boats are lying below the concessions out of range of Revolutionists' guns.

Enlistment among the rebels is going on apace, and their present strength is estimated to be about 25,000 men.

Celebrations in United States
San Francisco, Saturday—Dr. Sun Yat Sen, the Chinese revolutionary leader, has, through the agency of the Young China Association, directed that mass meetings and parades shall be held to-morrow throughout the United States, to celebrate the successes of the Chinese Revolutionaries. The American press is unable to ascertain the whereabouts of Dr. Sun Yat Sen. The Revolutionists say a sum of £40,000 has been collected for the Revolutionist cause among Chinese in the United States.

A Remarkable Insurrection
If we are not dulled by the suggestion of remoteness which always belongs in the mind of ordinary Western readers to Chinese names, and if we bring a little imagination to bear upon the matter we shall see that this movement in energy, scale, and dramatic character is one of the most notable things that the modern world has known, writes the "Observer." The present insurrection differs from the Taiping in the deliberate judgement and organised method with which it has so far been conducted. The lives and property of foreigners have been carefully protected. Missionaries have been treated with especial respect: so far not the shadow of an excuse has been given for foreign interference. This is remarkable enough as suggesting that the movement is not only the result of pre-preparation, but is under strong control.

Larne Times, Saturday, 21 October 1911

Dr Sun Yat-sen in Canton, 1924.

to show for the experience. Unlike the tough commanders who became his indispensable surrogates later in life, soldiering did not consume his life—literature and poetry did.

Always an avid reader, Mao's erudition and natural curiosity made him receptive to liberal ideas passed down from translated books and essays. By the time he was in his twenties, he had absorbed the Chinese intellectual's disdain for the country's backwardness, poverty and traditional customs. Venting his progressive ideas on paper, Mao flourished as an occasional contributor to the magazine *New Youth* run by two radicals, Li Dazhao and Chen Duxiu, and soon turned to publishing himself. In 1919, he was credited as the founder, editor and sole writer of the short-lived *Xiang River Review*, which was a personal project to collect his musings on current events.

There were other events in Mao's life that preoccupied him more than idle thoughts of becoming a rebel thinker. Brief interludes as a teacher, university assistant, occasional poet, and newlywed husband had little bearing on the turning point that awaited him in 1920 when a close friend, Cai Hesen, convinced him to turn communist.

The following year, Mao travelled to Shanghai for a rare summit. In attendance were the editors of *New Youth* and numerous radicals. Joining them was the Dutchman Henricus Sneevliet, whose earlier achievements included fomenting communist subversion in Java. It was rumoured that no less than Lenin had sanctioned his travel to China.

On 12 July 1921 the CCP was formed. It had the bare outline of an organization and a mandate to spread its influence far and wide. Its operating principle was to set the conditions for a communist takeover and impose a new regime over China, just like the one being established over what was formerly Czarist Russia. Mao did have a role to play in this unfolding drama, but it was a small one, and would remain so for a while.

While the 1920s are often remembered as a moment's relief in an otherwise turbulent half-century, China had it the worst among the world's great nations, for it had ceased to be one. It was reduced, catastrophically and geographically, to a rump state. Whereas the Qing Dynasty, assembled by Manchu conquerors between 1620 and 1644 from the wreckage of the earlier Ming Dynasty, grew into the last great Asian empire, encompassing the Korean peninsula, the Sinkiang deserts and the Tibetan plateau, not much was left of republican China.

Its most prosperous cities had to accommodate foreign cantonments. Since 1895, industrialized Japan with its modern army had annexed Formosa and Korea, and were creeping over the northern Manchurian provinces. The Mongols, Tibetans and the Turkmen enjoyed nominal independence along the frontiers. What remained truly Chinese were its central and southern provinces, which had no single regime to govern them as a whole country.

This dismayed Sun Yat-sen, now ailing from old age. The Nationalist party he established, alternately known as the Guomindang or Kuomintang, was a pariah on the world stage, and couldn't

Mao Zedong, 1935.

even field a proper army. For lack of trustworthy allies and a viable civil society to enhance its power, the KMT welcomed the newly minted communists, whose membership was ballooning. A year after their founding in Shanghai, the CCP arranged a partnership with the beleaguered KMT in what it dubbed the 'United Front'. The growing clout of the Chinese Communists was further enhanced by aid from the Soviet Union, the only country to lend the KMT unconditional support. This informal alliance blossomed in 1924 when Soviet advisers helped establish the Whampoa Military Academy, an institution whose sole aim was organizing modern Chinese armed forces trained to Western standards. At the opening of the academy, Sun Yat-sen said to the students: "My only hope in establishing this academy is to create a revolutionary army to save China from her crisis. From now on, decide not to cherish the idea of becoming high officials or making big fortunes, but devote yourselves to the enterprise that saves the nation and her people, and become bold revolutionary soldiers."

From its classrooms emerged the National Revolutionary Army, officered by young commanders who had earned their stripes in the previous decade's civil war. Many were avowed communists. For example, Zhou Enlai and Zhu De would rise to prominence in the CCP so many years later, and even do battle against their fellow Whampoa alumni.

Sun passed away in 1925 with little to show for his efforts at shepherding China toward a national rejuvenation. With the KMT on the brink of collapse as a result of losing their founder, the NRA hoisted Whampoa's superintendent, Chiang Kai-shek, to the party leadership in Canton, their de facto capital. But, like Sun and Yuan before him, the lack of a clear mandate left Chiang no choice but to impose his leadership by force. Far from a democrat with deeply held liberal beliefs, Chiang grew up in the waning years of the Qing era, and had trained in a Japanese military academy. He fully understood his country's weakness and thought himself foremost a strongman, a necessary arch-warlord who would use nationalism and social reform to cement his grip on power. But first, his enemies needed to be crushed.

By the end of 1925, Chiang had assembled an army 85,000 strong, equipped with modern arms. This force was divided into three: the First Army Corps, the Second Army Corps, and the Seventh Army Corps, led by experienced warlord generals. A year of preparation was needed to bolster the different corps with professional junior officers and stockpile supplies.

Troubled China

Russians to be Driven Out
Peking, Thursday: Official telegrams state that General Chang Kai Shek [sic], assisted by Mr C. C. Wu and other prominent Chinese, has effected a coup d'état in Canton, imprisoning Chinese and Russian Communists. Several Russians are reported to have been killed.—Reuter.

Red Generals Break Away
Shanghai, Thursday: Foreign despatches from Canton report a split in the Communist party there. A conflict occurred on Monday last between the party of the Generalissimo, Chiang Kaishek [sic], and the Chinese and Russian Communists, who, it is stated, have been striving to secure Chiang's election.

Chiang has now arrested some of the strike leaders and several Russians at the Whampao Cadet School, and is said to have decided to drive out all Russians and Communists from Canton.

Note—Mr C. C. Wu, who, in an earlier message from Peking, was stated to be assisting General Chiang, is the principal of the Whampao Cadet School.

The Retreating "National" Armies
Peking, Thursday: General Lu Chung-iin and Ming-chung now hold the dual command of the defeated Kuominchun (National) Army, which has been driven from Tientsin by the "Allied" General Li Chung-lin.

General Li Chung-lin is a rugged uncompromising fighter, and seems inclined to make the strong rearguard positions, held by the Kuominchun troops around Peking, into the scene of a decisive battle, although his colleagues are opposed to such a plan.

Meanwhile the Kuominchun authorities are striving desperately to find money to pay the great bodies of troops concentrated near the capital.—Reuter.

Hull Daily Mail, Thursday, 25 March 1926

On 7 July 1926, a new chapter began for China as the NRA undertook the historic Northern Expedition. Its goal was nothing less than to bring the provinces beyond the Yangtze valley under the KMT's control.

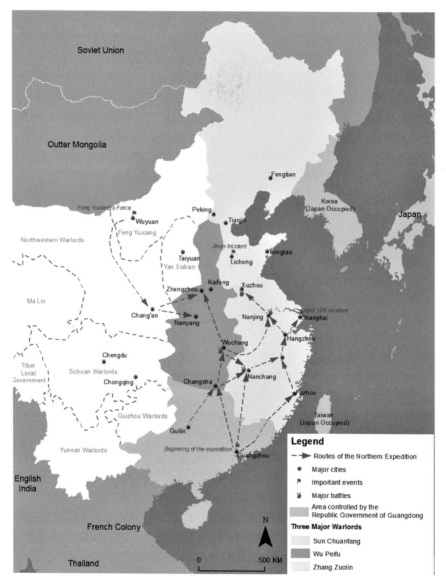

Northern Expedition, the military campaign launched by the Kuomintang in 1926. (Image Sy)

It was unclear if the Northern Expedition could achieve a satisfactory outcome, but its gains against the warlord armies were overshadowed by a political crisis within the KMT's ranks. With Chiang preoccupied with orchestrating the campaign, a revolt was brewing among the NRA's more seditious members.

The communists resented Chiang's rise to power as it echoed the tyranny of the late Yuan Shikai. Even worse for the communists, before launching the Northern Expedition, Chiang had assumed the role of commander-in-chief of the armed forces, including the miniscule navy and air corps. This allowed him to rule by decree on all matters related to his unification campaign. Such inordinate amount of executive leeway almost left the KMT's ruling Central Committee based in Canton helpless by comparison. If Chiang managed to subdue the northern provinces and seize the Qing's imperial capital Peiping, would he still bother establishing a true republican government?

Chiang did turn on the communists—eventually. By 1927, the lacklustre efforts by Soviet advisers in the Northern Expedition, coupled with rumours of communist plots to overthrow him, led to a purge within the KMT. Most damning was evidence found within the Soviet embassy in Peiping by a warlord's henchmen. Pamphlets, telegrams and arms were collected linking the embassy's staff to Comintern operatives and their local cells. Barely six years since their founding, the CCP and its thousands of members knew its days were numbered.

China's communists retaliated by orchestrating revolts in every major city controlled by the KMT. This doomed the Northern Expedition into a punitive exercise as Chiang and his generals scrambled to restore order. But the CCP's greatest coup didn't occur until August. On the first of the month, NRA regiments, led by communist sympathizers, mutinied and set about to establish a Soviet—a self-governing enclave—in the southern provinces of Jiangxi, Zhejiang and Fujian. At the forefront of the rebellion were Whampoa alumni who had combat experience in the civil war years, and, under their direction, the mutineers marched on the city of Nanchang and held fast.

So disastrous were the implications of the Nanchang revolt that the KMT nearly spiralled to its doom. Chiang himself, fed up with his country's treacherous politics, ceased the Northern Expedition and left for Japan on 12 August, determined to remain in exile there. But Nanchang was the CCP's first great defeat. KMT forces converged on the city and drove out the rebels. The communist threat dissipated before month's end and the CCP was reduced to an outlaw movement.

Among the survivors of the Nanchang débâcle was Zhu De, a hardy peasant who had risen through the NRA ranks. Having studied military science in Europe and the Soviet Union, his desertion from the NRA's ranks was a blow to its talent pool. But Zhu had been an ardent communist for years and the Nanchang battle was supposed to foment another revolution that would secure the CCP's dominion over China. It failed, not for lack of effort, but due to the unforeseen possibility that the CCP's message and methods were resented by China's urban populace.

This manifested in each province where the communists tried seizing the local capital. Despite claiming to represent the workers and the proletariat, their penchant for violence inspired violent resistance from the very citizens they tried winning over. With no other thought but survival, Zhu De and a few thousand diehards trekked across Jiangxi, where they knew a small soviet was established far from the KMT's wrath.

The Jiangxi Soviet began with less than a thousand members under Mao Zedong's command. Their little fiefdom actually straddled the borders of Jiangxi and Hunan, but its territorial reach was mostly confined to the Jinggangshan Mountains. Mao, still a low-ranking communist in his mid-1930s, was tasked with fomenting unrest in his home province, Hunan. Whether or not he succeeded in his mission

National Revolutionary Army (Nationalist) generals, Northern Expedition.

remains debatable. A large peasantry burdened by rents to the landowning class had long been a source of social conflict in the province. During the bitter years of the Taiping Rebellion from 1850 to 1865, Hunan numbered among the rogue territories that defied the Qing. In 1927, however, unprecedented rioting and skirmishes erupted as armed peasants attacked their landlords and tried redistributing privately owned estates.

While Mao could have earned his stripes as an agitator and mastermind behind the arson visited on Hunan's rural landowners, there is little evidence that he alone was responsible for the carnage. It was another event in late 1927 that was mythologized as Mao's first true revolutionary assault on the status quo. Enlisting the help of local miners and peasants, what became known as the Autumn Harvest Uprising, was sprung on 9 September to carve out a soviet within Hunan.

But the revolt was such a magnificent failure that Mao had to flee for his life and find shelter in neighbouring Jiangxi, where the old temples in Jinggangshan were turned into accommodation for Mao's pathetic little army of stragglers. Numbering just a few hundred, with scarcely enough firearms and ammunition, the origins of the Jiangxi Soviet marked the wilderness years for Mao, whose political skills were honed in the struggle to survive in a remote location constantly at risk of being attacked.

But Mao was no strategist—the dismal results of the Autumn Harvest Uprising was proof enough—and neither did he have a strong foundation in logistics and guerrilla warfare. He did compensate with a flair for bargaining and compromise. An early breakthrough in Jinggangshan was Mao's success at convincing a local bandit army to join his cause, a stroke of carefully engineered good fortune that increased his manpower to over a thousand armed fighters. Though still short of weapons, at least the soviet could protect itself from angry peasant militias.

In April 1928, the survivors of the Nanchang revolt, with Zhu De at their head, reached Jinggangshan and were absorbed into Mao's growing army. The two commanders recognized the value of fortifying Jinggangshan and using it as a base for expanding their influence over two provinces. Zhu De was prudent enough not to challenge Mao's authority and subordinated himself to Mao's leadership. This was another boon for the fledgling soviet, since its martial activities could then be delegated to an experienced commander while the administration remained in Mao's hands.

An enduring but pernicious myth surrounding the Jiangxi Soviet period is the rise of Mao's strategic genius. This was far from the truth. While the Jiangxi Soviet did overcome its growing pains, and thrive as a refuge for the embattled CCP, this was the result of so many NRA defectors who didn't hesitate to join in. By the 1930s, there were more than three dozen commissars and generals who helped organize thousands of peasants into what was first known as the Workers' and Peasants' Revolutionary Army, and then just the Red Army.

The Red Army's rapid expansion also invited enormous risk. Chiang Kai-shek returned to power in December 1927 and was hailed as China's generalissimo. With the failure of the Northern Expedition behind him, he focused his energies on repairing the country's stature and silencing dissent. A perpetual thorn in

Soldiers of the First Workers' and Peasants' Army, forerunner of the PLA, sorting grenades, during the Sino-Japanese War.

his side were the communists. Nearly eliminated in 1927, they had since broken apart to form petty soviets in different provinces. Jiangxi in particular was in danger of falling to the Red Army occupying Jinggangshan. Preoccupied with modernizing the NRA with the help of German advisers, Chiang first depended on warlord armies to conduct extermination campaigns. Unfortunately, from 1931 to 1933 four separate attempts to drive out the Jiangxi Soviet ended in failure. These defeats not only galvanized the Red Army in Jinggangshan, whose numbers had now swelled to more than 20,000 men and women, but became their leading source of arms. Warlord armies were so unreliable they often abandoned quantities of rifles, machine guns, ammunition and food after being ambushed and overrun.

In late 1933, however, Chiang sent a massive army into Jiangxi, supported from the air by bombers. A new strategy was employed too. The goal was to create rings of earthworks and bunkers that would restrict communist guerrillas' manoeuvring room and impose a siege on them. This methodical approach was carried out for almost a year, proving effective in diminishing the Red Army's ability to prosecute a war.

With a crushing defeat looming, Mao's grip on power in Jinggangshan was at risk. A plan was hastily drawn to preserve the Red Army and seek a new area for a soviet. Thousands of porters, along with horses and mules, were recruited to haul food, ammunition and office equipment essential to the soviet's propaganda machinery. The great trek commenced in October 1934, as 100,000 men, women and children, soldiers and peasants alike, evacuated Jinggangshan and its surrounding area in a southward migration.

Forming three enormous columns known as 'Front Armies', the brutal exodus traced a path right across Hunan's underbelly, braving the rough terrain of Guangxi and Guizhou. Many fell ill and perished in the southern jungles; many others were killed by pursuing NRA forces.

The logistical feat, celebrated as the 'Long March', saw the bulk of the Red Army and its political apparatus travel across a dozen provinces, under constant threat from either the KMT's aircraft or hostile locals. While there were a few engagements, later mythologized for propaganda purposes—the desperate Luding Bridge crossing does come to mind—these were usually skirmishes of little consequence with no clear victor. The communists spent months wandering between Guizhou and Yunnan, utterly lost. They traced the edge of Tibet's forbidding mountains and trudged barren wastes.

War to "Expirtate" a State

Fate of China's Soviet State

Shanghai: Threequarters of a million Chinese are directly involved in a desperate campaign on the result of which hangs the fate of the "Chinese Soviet Republic."

This development in China's internal convulsions is a state in the Kiangsi [Jiangxi] Province, 250 miles West of Shanghai, and controls a mountainous region about half the size of England with a population of five millions.

The Soviet is in the hands of some 400 young Chinese who have studied Communism in Moscow and Habarovsk [Khabarovsk]. Their rule is a challenge to the old civilisation of China. They are striving to abolish private enterprise and the influence of the family. Their regime is said to be enforced by terrorism.

At their capital, Juiking, resides the Central Commissioner, appointed by the Executive Council of the Communist Party in China.

A "Lenin" School

There a Communist daily newspaper is published. A "Lenin" school has been founded, and a "military and political institute" trains officers and commissars.

In the towns ... shops are run on a Soviet or co-operative basis, employees being on equal terms with their employers. All prices are State-controlled so as to eliminate private profit and enterprise.

The "workers and peasants' Red Army," under Cau The, musters 70,000 men. They are uniformed, well-armed, and possess plenty of machine guns. But their home-made powder is reported to be of poor quality. Washerwomen, guides, carrier coolies, and stretcher-bearers have been organised to follow them throughout the campaign.

They are preceded into action by a uniformed, but badly-armed, "Red Protection Army" numbering 100,000 men. These fighters, bearing spears, knives or bayonets, are conscripted from the peasantry and used as skirmishers.

Belfast News-Letter, Monday, 18 December 1933

Luding Bridge over the Dadu River, Sichuan Province, China. (Photo fsyzh)

An entire year passed before Mao and a column of survivors reached Shanxi, an impoverished province so far away from Chiang's capital Nanking, that it helped diminish the threat posed by the KMT. Short on everything except physical labour, the battered Red Army utilized crude shelters dug out from barren hillsides. Other remnants from the Long March arrived in 1935. Most of those who had joined at the beginning had died. Numerous accounts later claimed just 30,000 half-starved communists had made it to their new home. Chiang himself believed there were fewer than 20,000 left.

The Long March was the single worst defeat endured by the CCP. It was, without a doubt, their lowest ebb. If it had a silver lining, it was to guarantee the leadership survived along with their commanders. It also benefited Mao, who cemented his grip on the entire movement during the exodus. This marked his ultimate rise as the undisputed leader of Chinese Communism.

Outlaws at Panopa, Xinjiang. Autonomous warlords added considerable confusion to the revolution. (Photo M. A. Stein via Ralph Repo)

Once ensconced in a remote corner of Shanxi, Mao's rebels had breathing room and a safe haven from which to rebuild. Years later, after almost a decade spent in his dusty fortress, Mao was visited by a British university lecturer named Robert Young, who wished to size him up. Mao was already considered a legend at the time, a cross between a sage and a zealot. When Young was finally introduced, he would recall: "There was about him a kind of quietness such as you will find among people who have lived much alone ... he was 53 and looked 20."

Revolutionary artillery in action. (Image Charles Somerville via Ashley Van Haeften)

2. SHADOW OF THE RISING SUN

The Second Sino-Japanese War of 1937–1945, was actually the bloodiest phase of a long struggle for the Chinese heartland. Thirty years prior, the empire of Japan had already turned Manchuria into an outpost.

The gifts of the twentieth century were too generous to the empire of Japan. An archipelago of three main volcanic islands, prone to earthquakes and with little arable land and no fossil fuel deposits, Japanese industriousness created a population boom that grew year on year. As an Asian power with a Prussian cast imposed by its constitution, a convivial and democratic outlook on national life never figured in political discourse.

When China was engulfed by civil strife after 1911, Japan had mastered economic planning on a foundation of coal, railroads and factories. Korea was its

Japanese soldiers of the Sino-Japanese War, 1895

offshore base for cheap labour. This was not enough, for Japan needed to be stronger, even unassailable. Beyond its waters was the Korean peninsula, and across the Yalu River lay Manchuria, vast and ripe for annexation.

Manchuria was an exciting, rugged and unforgiving place. The history of its land and people are unknown. Until the twentieth century, Western travellers could only marvel at its geography and weather. Manchuria's ill-defined borders were the Yalu River with Korea, and the Yellow Sea to the south. To the east and north were the Usuri and Amur rivers, the natural boundaries separating it from Russia, where the steppes merged with the tundra and taiga. To the west were Mongolia's grasslands.

At the end of the First Sino-Japanese War in 1895, Manchuria was coveted by Russia as the last piece of its Siberian domain. With the blessing of France and Germany, Russia was able to position herself as China's defender, seizing Port Arthur and keeping Manchuria out of Japanese clutches.

At the end of the Russo-Japanese War, that saw Tokyo victorious, Manchuria was available for the taking. Japan could not move in, however, since this could provoke another conflict. The stratagem that best suited its designs was a cunning one. If modernization had a single impetus, it was the cycle of accumulating and investing capital. Japan had perfected modernization. Now it needed a clean slate to invest with its capital.

According to Louis Livingston Seaman, MD, veteran of the Spanish-American War and the Boxer Rebellion, Japan's arrival in mainland China boded well for the future. Writing in 1905, he praised the Japanese army and navy as models of efficiency.

Dr Seaman insisted their presence was needed to stop an imperialist Russia: "It would indeed be a peril and terror to civilization were these hardy peasants of Manchuria and the countless hordes of China transformed into minions of the White Czar."

Nine years before the First World War, and long before the Treaty of Versailles and its limitations on the imperial Japanese navy's tonnage, Dr Seaman believed that Japan acted as a regional balancer. He continued: "The main present hope of security against this lies in a complete victory of the patriots of the Land of the Rising Sun, which shall effectually stem the tide of Russian aggression for this generation at least, thus giving China one more chance to 'put her house in order'."

Seaman was earnest in his best wishes for China, then the proverbial sick man of Asia. "So long as England, Japan, and our own land [the United States] stand

Russia and Manchuria

The mists concealing Russian proceedings in eastern Asia are gradually dissolving. All the same, it is noteworthy that the St. Petersburg censorship actually allows the "Novosti" [lit. news] to make known how extensive are the Czar's warlike preparations of the Manchurian frontier.

The outside world was previously aware that strong reinforcements were being almost continuously dispatched from the Black Sea to Vladivostok. But our contemporary adds the interesting information that a similar flow of fighting strength has been setting towards Manchuria ever since last May. In artillery alone, the augmentation already amounts to six batteries, and, no doubt, more will follow in due course.

The "Novosti" explains, as it was, of course, bound to do, that these apparently menacing measures have no other purpose than the protection of the Amur region from Japanese invasion.

Remembering that there are already 90,000 Russian soldiers at and near Vladivostok, a force amply sufficient to defend the frontier even if the Japanese meditated attack, there can be no doubt whatever that the Czar has some widely different object in view ... the bringing down of the eastern extremity of the Siberian railway to the Gulf of Pe-chi-li, and the creation there of a Russian arsenal, and strongly fortified naval port. Once that position is attained, the Czar will have tight hold on the throat of the Asiatic "sick man" [China].

Globe, Friday, 4 October 1895

pat for the integrity of this great unwieldy empire, the machinations of her foes will assuredly be circumvented," he wrote.

Perhaps what was beyond Seaman's ability to foresee was how sinister the Imperial Japanese Army's administration of Manchuria would become. In the ensuing decades they turned it into a colony with its very own state-within-a-state, the Kwantung Army. In the following years, its control of the region grew exponentially. So much so, that this mutation of Japan's borders, which now spread across East Asia, created dangerous strains that paved the way for its eventual defeat in the Second World War. Despite its ominous name, the Kwantung Army

Japanese army crushes the Manchu Army, by artist Yoshu Chikanobu.

began as a small garrison, tasked with protecting the Japanese-owned railroads that transported Manchurian produce and raw materials to Korea. But as time went on its size and role began to change. With the benefit of hindsight and historical records, it appears the Kwantung Army's distance from Tokyo made its officers more autonomous, more daring and reckless.

On 4 June 1928, the Chinese warlord Zhang Zhuo-lin was assassinated by a bomb planted in his railway car. This early attempt to subvert Manchuria was inconclusive. Three years later, the Kwantung Army overran Manchuria. On 18 September 1931, a bomb blast on the South Manchurian Railway was blamed on Chinese forces, leading to further military action. The resulting war was brief, but it devastated Shanghai and saw the loss of China's three northernmost provinces, which were to form Japan's colony of Manchukuo. It was a daring endeavour to found an industrial colony on China's unforgiving frontier. The deposed Qing emperor, Puyi, was even rustled out of his post-imperial life to serve as nominal head of state.

All the years of subterfuge and belligerence in northeastern China were minor acts in a grander drama. The Kwantung Army needed to be secure and impervious should the day come when the rival Soviet Red Army might come crashing down the steppes, across the Amur River, and into the intended bread-basket of Japan.

As the Kwantung Army and its officers went about the task of colonizing Manchuria, the Imperial Japanese Army (IJA) and navy were making preparations for the next war. What is often missed when assessing Japan's national character before the war is that the political and military leadership were often at odds.

Preparations for this momentous struggle had been underway for years. When the US War Department commissioned studies on Japan's military, what these publications revealed was an efficient fighting machine with a vast arsenal. The IJA's air service had thousands of trained pilots and aircraft. Their navy was the best in the eastern hemisphere. The Japanese infantryman, airman and sailor were formed in the same mould. No matter the branch, training was exacting, harsh and literally painful. The Japanese soldier was often portrayed as a yellow-skinned, bow-legged malefactor, but, in reality, he was a young man who was routinely punished, beaten and humiliated by his superiors.

But he had an excellent rifle in the 6.5mm Model 38 that was later replaced by the more powerful 8mm Model 94, colloquially known as the Arisaka. The IJA's apparel was tough and the hand grenades issued to the infantry were diverse and lethal.

Japanese infantrymen also had a quaint muzzle-loaded 50mm grenade discharger for intermediate ranges, as well as a semi-automatic 20mm anti-tank rifle.

Mk A 'Whippets' in Japanese service in Manchuria, early 1930s.

Japanese patrol, 1937.

A lethal variety of machine guns and mortars was available to IJA companies. A new range of tankettes and light tanks, as well as towed artillery, was introduced in the 1930s.

In comparison, by 1937 the Kuomintang's National Revolutionary Army (NRA) was in questionable shape. After the departure of Soviet advisers in 1927, the NRA turned to German veterans of the Great War. Most prominent were an unspecified number of Germans, including Colonel General Hans von Seeckt, who had fought the Russians on the Eastern Front. Von Seeckt and a succession of officers gave Chiang Kai-shek a well-trained and highly motivated corps of 300,000 men by 1936. Added to this were between 900,000 and a million auxiliaries. Thanks to foreign aid, the NRA had access to a modern, albeit limited, arsenal. Small arms like the 7.92mm Mauser 98K and the 8.5mm vz 26 machine gun gave the NRA infantry top-of-the-line firepower.

Chiang's "Fight On" call from his Field H.Q.

From his field headquarters at Nanchang, some 300 miles south-west of Nanking, General Chiang Kai-shek yesterday broadcast this call to the nation:

"To capitulate is to court disaster ...

"No matter how the present situation may change, we must not surrender, but march onward."

He admitted that Chinese casualties on all fronts have exceeded 300,000, and "the loss to civilian life and property is beyond computation."

Confident

"We are convinced," he declared (quoted by Reuter), "that the present situation is favourable to China. On the basis of China's future success, prolonged resistance is not to be found in the big cities, nor in the big towns, but in the villages throughout China, and in the fixed determination of the people.

"The time must come when Japan's military strength will be completely exhausted, thus giving an ultimate victory."

While Chiang was making his appeal, the Japanese were planning a "triumphal march" into Nanking for to-day. With 200 planes roaring overhead, General Matsui, the Japanese Commander, will lead thousands of Japanese troops into the city.

Daily Herald, Friday, 17 December 1937

Limited amounts of modern artillery and light tanks, including French Renault FT-17s and Soviet T-26s also reached the NRA. On the eve of the Second Sino-Japanese War, the NRA was laying the groundwork for what would become the Republic of China air force. This time it was the Soviet Union that provided the hardware: some 500 propeller-driven light fighter aircraft and more than 300 bombers. The navy possessed modern gunboats and cruisers.

It took a bizarre turn of events to set the NRA and the IJA against each other. Two incidents—one in Shanghai and the other in the former Imperial capital Beijing—would spiral out of control and start an epic battle involving millions.

19th Route Army in an engagement with the Japanese on the Chapei front.

In July, units of the Kwantung Army seized Peiping's historic Marco Polo Bridge. In August, a Japanese navy officer was killed by Chinese sentries in Shanghai. There continues to be speculation that that NRA General Zhang Zhi-zhong— apparently a high-level Soviet agent—orchestrated the incident to provoke a war at the behest of Stalin.

The resulting three-month battle for Shanghai, from August 13 to November 19, was a futile one. In the span of a hundred days, the NRA was almost eliminated while the IJA had a rude awakening. The Chinese could put up a tremendous fight and rising Japanese casualties posed a threat to any invading force's momentum.

The KMT and its military had the worst of it, however. The IJA might have been slowed down, but the NRA's losses were in the hundreds of thousands. Gone were its best officers, half of the air corps, and most of its tanks and artillery. Meanwhile, the Kwantung Army in the north had seized Peiping and Inner Mongolia.

Chiang Kai-shek's options were poor ones. With the national armed forces in disarray and the IJA on the march, on 1 December 1937, the KMT abandoned their

19th Route Army defending a makeshift position in Shanghai.

capital Nanjing, known to Europeans as Nanking, and made Wuhan the temporary capital. Meanwhile, the NRA general tasked with defending Nanjing, Tang Sheng-zhi, had the manpower at his disposal, but not the will or strategy to block the oncoming IJA. So, Nanking fell and its inhabitants were at the mercy of the IJA. What followed was a grim and baffling period that has echoed down the years to haunt Japan to the present day.

From 13 December until the end of January the following year, foreign missionaries and members of the diplomatic community witnessed the wanton arson and looting by Japanese soldiers. A week before, the retreating Kuomintang tried to destroy any structures of value lest these be captured by the IJA. Now entire neighbourhoods were razed and civilians were being rounded up. Soon the killing began. What has baffled historians since is that the atrocities perpetrated in Nanking had no precedent and seemed to have had little purpose other than to inflict cruelty on its citizens.

But primary sources are also available. The earliest testimonies on Nanking during the first two months of Japanese occupation came from two unlikely

"Annihilation" of the Nanking Garrison

"The virtual annihilation of the Chinese garrison at Nanking is considered merely a question of hours," it was stated in Tokio this morning.

This afternoon came a message that the "complete occupation" of Nanking at sunset had been announced by the Japanese. Previous news had revealed that Japanese troops had captured all the gates in the southern and eastern walls of Nanking, and had also taken Chinese positions near the historic Ming Tombs.

Although still resisting furiously, the Chinese defending Nanking were being slowly driven back and suffering heavy casualties.

Among the buildings of Nanking occupied by the Japanese, according to Japanese reports, are General Chiang Kai-Shek's house, the headquarters of the Military Academy, and the National Government Office.

The remnants of the Chinese troops, who offered so stiff a resistance on the Purple Mountain, which dominates Nanking, have been wiped out by a fire which the Japanese started at the base of the mountain last night. In two hours the slopes were enshrouded in flames.

Hull Daily Mail, Monday, 13 December 1937

American conspirators: Reverend John Magee and George Fitch, the head of the local YMCA. Together they would smuggle 16mm footage out of China. The footage caught Japanese atrocities in and around the International Safety Zone, where they vainly tried to save as many as they could.

It was brave but futile. Constantly harassed by the Japanese, Fitch and a small group of foreigners, including the heroic German ambassador John Rabe, bore witness to the IJA's revenge on Nanking. Fitch kept a journal of his experiences. Hardly four days after the IJA stormed the city, were mass rapes being perpetrated.

"Over a hundred women that we knew of were taken away by soldiers," Fitch wrote. 'Refugees were searched for money and anything they had on them was taken away, often to their last bit of bedding. It was a day of unspeakable horror ..."

Fitch recalls the story of a Chinese man he tried saving: "He was one of a gang of some hundred who had been tied together, then gasoline was thrown over them and set fire."

Imperial Japanese Army troops in Nanjing where they massacred as many as 300,000 Chinese.

Women were fair game. Japanese soldiers would break into homes, steal anything of value, and then take turns raping them. Sometimes the women were killed, sometimes not. Eight days before Christmas Eve 1937, Fitch wrote, "A rough estimate at least would be a thousand women raped last night and during the day ... one poor woman was raped 37 times," he added. "Another had her five months infant deliberately smothered by the brute to stop its crying while he raped her."

There are no exact figures of civilian deaths in Nanking, or even deaths from the surrounding countryside—the Japanese burned every village on the outskirts of the capital. The numbers that have endured are large 'guesstimated' statistics. Allowing for a bare minimum of 50,000 civilians killed, would mean that the IJA had murdered at least 1,200 men and women every day for six weeks. It could also have been 300,000 civilians killed, meaning killed by bayonet, by beating, by gun shot, by fire, or by sword. Decapitated. Impaled. Robbed and murdered. What cannot be denied or cast in doubt was the scale of Japanese brutality.

It could also have been 600,000 civilians killed. How many were women raped first and then disposed of?

Aside from the 16mm film Fitch smuggled in his overcoat to Shanghai and then to the US with the help of McGee, photographs survive of mutilated corpses, pyramids of severed heads, of women stripped bare and taken for trophies.

The IJA also looted Nanking. The value of this wealth has been forgotten by history. In the face of this carnage, the mistaken bombing of the gunboat USS *Panay* that killed two Americans and an Italian journalist is, understandably, a footnote. For this incident the Japanese government apologized and paid reparations. One of the ugliest consequences of the Nanking massacre was the institutionalization of prostitution across IJA-occupied territories. Once the system was up and running in China, in the coming years the same would be done in the Philippines, Vietnam, the Dutch Indies, and even Korea.

There were other battles in the Second Sino-Japanese War larger than Shanghai and Nanking. Throughout, China's generals would always miscalculate and err, bungling their operations despite the largesse of foreign aid and expertise.

In August 1939, with the Chinese reeling after three years of savage warfare, the IJA would embark on its last northern adventure. The goal was the same as before, to expand the boundaries of Manchukuo. But the consequences were dire. In a place the Soviets called Khalkhin-Gol, whole IJA divisions were encircled and wiped out by a methodical, combined arms operation led by a former cavalryman named Georgi Zhukov. The Japanese soldier, tough as he was, was outfought.

Battle at the Great Wall, Liaoyuan, Hebei, autumn 1937.

Simply put, the Soviets had better artillery, more tanks, and a lethal new doctrine that annihilated infantry formations. After Khalkhin-Gol, also known as Nomonhan, the IJA had no stomach to fight the Soviets. Manchukuo and the Kwantung Army's fate was sealed on 9 August 1945 when two great pincers of the Red Army swept through northern China.

Chiang Resigns as P.M.

To Concentrate on Jap War

Generalissimo Chiang Kai-Shek resigned today as President of the Executive Yuan (Premier) to devote himself to the Jap war. He is succeeded by the Acting Premier, Mr. T.V. Soong, says Spenser Moosa, Associated Press correspondent, in a message from Chungking [Chongqing].

The elevation of Mr. Soong to the full Premiership raised the possibility that he might attend any impending meeting of the Big Five. It would also give him greater face if he makes the unexpected visit to Moscow on his way to China from San Francisco.

Main Job

Chiang's relinquishment of the post of Premier does not affect his position as President of China and head of the State.

Chiang announced his resignation at a meeting of the newly elected Executive Committee of the Kuomintang, the National People's Party. It is presumed that Chiang, in view of the accelerated tempo of the Far Eastern war, intends to devote himself primarily to his main job—Supreme Commander of the Allied Forces in the China theatre.

Mr. Soong, Acting Premier since December 4, 1944, attended to most of Chiang's duties as Premier. His transition from Acting Premier, therefore, is not surprising, and, in fact, had been expected in Chungking for some time. As Premier, Mr. Soong will probably be in a better position to talk to Marshal Stalin in the matter of improving relations between China and Russia.

Liverpool Evening Express, Thursday, 31 May 1945

Kwantung Army Yields

The Japanese Kwantung Army Group formally surrendered in Harbin yesterday to Major-general Shelakhov, cables Reuter's special correspondent from Moscow today. This much vaunted Army died ingloriously in 13 days, from losses and retreats on three fronts.

It died of disorganisation caused by the rapid advance of the Red Armies in front of it, and by the spreading of revolts of the Manchurians in its rear.

The power of what Japan has proclaimed to be "the flower of their Samurai" lies strewn across steppes and mountains, and along roads and railways—abandoned and smashed equipment, ruined fortifications ... and rows of blackened corpses.

The Soviet officers found that when the group surrendered that the rot had gone so far that the H.Q. was unable to communicate with all the fleeing divisions, and that so far it had been impossible to send them news of the surrender.

That is why fighting still continues.

"Wolves" Still Prowling

Scattered remnants of the Japanese armies who refused to surrender, called by the Russians "steppe wolves," are prowling in the interior of Manchuria, harassing Soviet communications and outposts, and terrorising Chinese villages and farms.

Their appearance was planned by the Japanese Command. They are desperate and dangerous, well-armed, and carrying their own food.

They often disguise themselves as Chinese civilians, and sometimes put on Red Army uniforms. Specially formed highly mobile Soviet forces are hunting them down.

Isolated Japanese groups are continuing to resist in some of the Sakhalin fortifications.

Gloucestershire Echo, Wednesday, 22 August 1945

The Sixth Kuomintang Party Congress that convened 5 May that year set policies that would have a profound effect on all aspects of life in China over

Elite German-trained troops of the National Revolutionary Army before the Battle of Wuhan, 1938.

the next five years. The KMT identified the fundamental imperative to meet strong domestic and foreign demands for constitutional government in China without diluting or yielding power to other Chinese political parties through the formation of a coalition government.

The election of a new Central Executive Committee (CEC), the scheduling of a Constitutional Assembly, and the adoption of resolutions for far-reaching social reforms had to conform to party policy. However, even the possibility of a redistribution of factional control within the KMT was negated when the Central Club, or 'CC', clique and its right-wing allies swept the CEC vote. The Chinese Communists and the Chinese Democratic League immediately protested the decisions of the KMT congress, claiming that a truly democratic assembly could not be convened until all China's parties were legalized and nationwide elections held throughout China.

By design, but not by description, absolute authoritarian control of the KMT was enshrined in the Kuomintang Congress when in session. It was the supreme legal authority of the party, subject only to the veto of

National Revolutionary Army machine-gunners, c. 1939.

Chiang Kai-shek, who served as both KMT director-general and president of the Republic of China. The organization of Congress and the manner of selecting delegates to it were set by the CEC, the highest party organ when Congress itself was not in session.

With Congress usually only sitting every second year, the CEC was empowered to issue key policy directives and to elect the presidents and vice-presidents of the five administrative arms, or Yuans, of government: the Executive, Legislative, Judicial, Examination and Control.

Whilst the 731 Congress members were ostensibly elected from various regional and functional divisions of the party, in practice the delegates had to be approved by the Ministry of Organization. As a consequence, the reality was that candidates were frequently appointed as a result of political agreements and trade-offs between factions within the KMT.

With the prevailing instability, it had been impossible to hold normal party elections in more than a few areas of China. The CEC elected in 1938 had there-fore been able to appoint a disproportionate number of delegates to the May 1945 Congress, including many representing the Japanese-occupied provinces. As a result, factional allegiances and alignments within the Sixth Congress had already been determined in part by the ongoing struggle for power.

Although many of the elected delegates were said to be opposed to the 'CC' clique, they were outnumbered by appointees. Besides geographical representation, which included some overseas Chinese, the Congress received delegates from party organizations in various occupational and institutional categories such as universities, labour unions, factories and mines, and the army. The army delegation was evenly divided between supporters of the relatively moderate Minister of War General Chen Cheng and those of reactionary Chief of Staff General Ho Ying-chin.

Elections for the CEC, one of the principal items on the Congress agenda, were held for the first time since the Congress of 1938. The new organ, as the ruling body of the KMT in the crucial years ahead, would have to determine Chongqing (Chiang Kai-shek's provisional capital) policies on such vital issues as internal political unity and reform, and relations with the both Moscow and Washington. However, the recent 'elections' did little to change the complexion of the ranks of party power. Sun Fo and Madame Sun Yat-sen were retained, probably as window dressing of loyalty to the party's founder. Leaders of the 'CC' clique, brothers Guofu and Chen Chen Lifu, employed patronage and strong political organization to assure their continued control of the KMT, which could be sustained even after the new constitution was adopted.

The most serious threat to 'CC' domination of the KMT came from a coalition headed by war minister General Chen Cheng and education minister Chu Chia-hua, which was able to group together a strong loyal minority among the Congress delegates. This collaboration between the more liberal elements in the Chinese army and those civil government officials who were avidly opposed to the Chen brothers' hegemony, would remain a significant force in China's short-term political life.

Dominating the Congress was the awareness of a need to review the party's position in respect to China's unresolved political problems. The ruling elite regarded the strengthening of her armed forces as China's most urgent task to expedite the rapid destruction of the Japanese enemy. Congress emphasized that, thereafter, there was a need for continuing amicable relations with the United States, the United Kingdom, and the Soviet Union in global post-war reconstruction. Sino-Soviet cooperation was essential because of the long common frontier and many contacts between the two nations. Whilst harbouring no territorial ambitions, the Congress reconfirmed China's position stated in the Cairo Declaration calling for the restoration of Chinese territories lost to the Japanese and for the independence of Korea. In addition, resolutions favouring the conclusion of commercial treaties based on equality and reciprocity and the realization of local autonomy for Mongolia and Tibet were passed.

The most important act of the May Congress, table by President Chiang, was to set 12 November 1945 as the date for the national assembly to ratify China's draft constitution. The fealty of the assembly would be assured by the CEC's authority to determine its exact powers and membership, and in turn, by the 'CC' clique's total control of the CEC.

The national assembly, however, would not be a constituency-elected assembly in the Western style. Any powers the assembly exercised to amend the draft constitution, already unilaterally drawn up by Kuomintang leaders, would be curtailed by CEC directives. The draft constitution was sharply criticized by Chinese liberals for its virtual carte blanche appointive powers it vested in the president, who would not be chosen by popular vote but by an elected national assembly, and meeting only one month in every three years. In the final analysis, the constitution, once approved, would serve only to legitimize the de facto one-party, Kuomintang rule.

Chinese Communist leaders declared that they had not subscribed to such a constitutional government formed during the war, arguing that this would only consolidate and protect Chongqing's hold on power. They even ventured to suggest that, if the assembly sat in November, the KMT would also be preparing an excuse for civil war. The Congress resolution which promised that Chongqing would seek a 'political solution' to the Kuomintang–Communist stalemate contained no tangible proposals. The resolution stated that a settlement would be possible only "as long as the discussions do not adversely affect the progress of our war against aggression or endanger the state".

Generalissimo Chiang Kai-shek in full uniform, 1940s.

The May Congress also passed resolutions encompassing broad social reforms in compliance with Sun Yat-sen's third principle: the 'people's livelihood'. The meeting declared that the KMT favoured a very advanced social programme, which included a minimum wage scale, a 48-hour working week, tax reforms, and annual vacations with pay for Chinese farmers and labourers. Whilst the widespread publicity given the resolutions led many to believe that the KMT was about to launch a working-class social programme, the communists or the Democratic League were not convinced. There had been several occasions over the last twenty years that the KMT had passed similarly progressive legislation without ever implementing their promises. Commentators at the time dismissed the KMT's social resolutions as being no more than a gesture to advance an alternative and more attractive programme to the one offered by the Communist or the Democratic League parties.

Congress also appeared to strive toward the relinquishment by the KMT of much of its traditional power. A call was made for the abolition of party branches in the Chinese army and in schools, the election of municipal, county, and provincial councils to serve as full-fledged representative organs, enactment of a law legalizing other political parties, and the transfer to the government of party administrative departments such as the Ministry of Information. Seemingly, Chiang and the other party leaders wanted to make a show of terminating the period of political tutelage that Sun Yat-sen had prescribed to prepare China for constitutional democracy.

The Congress had been organized to be run from the top, so suggestions as to how the KMT leadership would operate under a constitution were quietly ignored. All acts of the body originated from the executive planners, so in-house reform agitation was effectively futile. To retain its grip on power, the party leadership strove to strengthen the KMT organization through substantial recruitment of competent political workers. In the absence of a solid, clear-cut programme for revising the land tenure and taxation systems, the KMT would not have much success in enlisting strong agrarian support. The KMT ruling elite had no intention of either instituting administrative reforms within the government, or substantial economic and political reforms that might give the party a popular grassroots base. It was, however, determined to pursue the perpetuation of a set of conventional administrative and political controls to maintain power, augmented by a drive to increase and extend party organization in the lower levels.

Chiang Kai-shek maintained a dominating influence over Congress proceedings, with reports indicating that he virtually dictated the committee elections

Eighty million Chinese Communists who inhabit thousands of square miles of northern China and are ruled, in spite of the Kuomintang, by Mao Zedong, December 1944. (Photo US NARA)

and passage of resolutions. Some of the more liberal delegates, particularly those followers of Sun Fo, raised objections against these tactics. However, the 'CC' clique's firm control and orchestration of proceedings prevented these criticisms from having any impact. It was later noted that as many as 450 delegate interpellations were made questioning the KMT regime's policies.

Newspapers in Free China gave considerable editorial cover to the KMT Congress, both before and during its convention. The KMTcontrolled press, whilst voicing expected laudatory conventional statements about the party, subtly hinted at its deteriorating position, urging that introspection was necessary for its rejuvenation. The *Central Daily News* declared that measures should be taken to maintain the Kuomintang as China's leading party, even under constitutional rule. After political power was restored to the people, the party had to still continue with its "duty of national reconstruction". The paper demanded that

The Rising Sun over
Nanking proclaims
victory.

"actions that cause a breach in the diplomatic, military, financial, communications, and currency unity of the country" had to be prohibited.

Meanwhile, independent newspapers spoke overtly and without apparent restraint on the pressing political and economic issues confronting both government and party. Calls were made for fresh, free democratic elections to the national assembly in November, and for modification of the nine-year-old draft constitution. The independents entreated for the relegation of the Kuomintang's status to that of a political party equal to all others. The *Ta Kung Pao* was blunt, openly declaring that seventeen years of unchecked KMT rule in China had been too long, and accusing the party of having failed to practise two of the three Sun Yat-sen principles relating to the people's power and the people's livelihood, opting to confine itself solely to the third principle of nationalism.

3. WASHINGTON AND MOSCOW

The surrender of Japan marked the pinnacle of prestige for nationalist leader Chiang Kai-shek personally, and of the regime under his control, a status enjoyed at home and abroad. Consecutive 'unequal treaties' in the course of a century had reduced China to quasi-semi-colonial status. The abolition of this state of affairs had been the principal purpose of the Nationalist Revolution. This had at last been swept away for all time in the aftermath of Pearl Harbor and Japanese imperial expansionism. The United States and Britain had welcomed China into the ranks of the Allies on terms of complete parity. In fact, in the final months of the war, the US had gone even further to insist, upon the establishment of the United Nations and in spite of the thinly veiled annoyance of Britain and the Soviet Union, that China's importance merited her official recognition as one of the five major powers, with a permanent seat on the UN Security Council with right of veto.

Unity of Strength. Chiang Kai-shek and Winston Churchill, with the Nationalist Chinese flag and the Union Flag.

These were certainly achievements that Chiang could be proud of, as reflected in the cities of eastern and northern China—Peiping, Shanghai and Nanking—which had been in Japanese hands for eight years, where the inhabitants were eagerly waiting to fete their liberator and hero. Chiang's triumph was made sweeter still by the absence in his camp of rivals to usurp his moment of glory. Wang Ching-Wei, who from the foundation of the National Government in 1927 had led numerous connivances against Chiang's authority, ultimately taking his group of dissenters over to the Japanese side in 1938. Wang himself had died in 1944, but for his disciples, all that remained was to pay the price of their treason.

However, upon closer analysis, the scenario was far less reassuring. For instance, Wang's gang of renegades had included many of the most competent nationalist administrators whose absence, already noticeable in declining government efficiency, would be even more conspicuous when it came to the issues of post-war rehabilitation. There could be no hiding the fact that the Chongqing administration was showing signs of incapacity that could not be accounted for simply by the weariness accrued from eight years of fighting. This period of combat had been spent in a remote and comparatively backward part of the country, far removed from the commerce and industry of the Lower Yangtse Valley which had provided the milieu for the brief halcyon days of Nationalist China before 1937.

It would not be Shanghai entrepreneurs but landowners of a pronounced reactionary ilk whose support had to be courted, so party policy was modified accordingly. In a culture of this traditional sort, in most cases industrial development tended to be instituted under official auspices, which, in turn significantly increased the scope for corruption.

The avarice of the so-called 'Four Great Families', a reactionary Kuomintang coalition that ruled China from 1927 through 1949, became legend. Headed by Chiang Kai-shek, the consortium was made up of members of the families of Chiang Kai-shek, Sung Tzu-wen, K'ung Hsiang-hsi and of the brothers Guofu and Chen Lifu. After seizing power and establishing their control over the country's monopolies, they subjected the Chinese people to unabashed and brutal exploitation. In twenty-two years of absolute power, they had accumulated assets in excess of $20 billion. The Four Families relied on the support of the imperialist powers, especially the US, whose position in Kuomintang China was noticeably strengthened. The example set by the Four Families percolated down into the humbler ranks in every department of China's public service.

Chiang Kai-shek, third from right, with senior KMT officers.

In sharp contrast, refugees from the occupied provinces, particularly teachers, whose status was so important in the traditional Chinese world, were in a most appalling condition, for inflation had reached enormous proportions. The result was that now, with the cessation of global hostilities, the disillusion and rancour throughout the areas controlled from Chongqing formed a striking contrast with the hero-worship in which Chiang was still basking among the population of occupied China, where for years his very name had been the epitome of national resistance.

The excesses of the Kuomintang regime were especially noticeable in its interaction with the communists. The tenuous alliance between the two parties had broken down from around the beginning of 1941 when the communist New Fourth Army on the Yangtse was attacked and dispersed by a Nationalist general. This engagement had been followed through to 1943 by a series of Japanese offensives against the communist areas in the northwest, into which it had been purported that Kuomintang troops had moved to support the invaders. Whatever the circumstances or veracity of such accusations, the communists suffered badly: the population under their control fell from 44 million to 25 million, while the strength of the Red Eighth Route Army was reduced from 400,000 to 300,000. However, by mid-1945, the communist-liberated region stretched across the whole width of the northern half of China to the coast, thereby blocking off Kuomintang forces from access to Peiping, Tientsin and Manchuria. Communist power was now stronger than it had ever been.

What was of almost equal significance were the fantastic legends to which these achievements spawned, for it was the stuff of fables that victory on such a scale could have been won despite a Kuomintang blockade of all external aid. Conversely, the nationalists could boast of no comparable successes in the field. It is acknowledged that, in the last weeks of the war, Chiang's forces had, with the assistance of considerable US air support, launched an offensive in the south, recovering, for example, the city of Kweilin. However, this victory was arguably to be attributed primarily to the Japanese need for retrenchment rather than to Kuomintang military capabilities.

Japanese army officers in China.

Although this period constitutes a profound seminal period in the formation of Maoist ideology, foreign, and particularly US, admiration of the communist war effort, enriched as it was by contrast with the ongoing ineptitude of the nationalists' performance, was not in any way tainted by any fears about the future. In fact, at the time Washington found that the very title 'Chinese Communists' was a ridiculous misnomer. Mao and his adherents, many State-side analysts pontificated, were no more than agrarian reformists whose political affiliations and dogma were, in western terms, right of centre.

This extraordinary misconception was probably enhanced by the decision of the communist leaders during the war to slow down the pace of their policy and to restrict their campaign against landlordism to the control of rents within reasonable limits, and by Mao's philosophy of 'New Democracy' which proposed close cooperation between the communists and all classes and parties against the Japanese presence.

Regardless of its origins, however, this perception of the Yenan regime as an organization of moderate democrats was widely fomented by an influential group of American Foreign Service officials. Though not accepted in its totality by Washington, nonetheless this formed part of the background to US government thinking. This process was further accommodated in August 1944 by the establishment of a US military mission in Yenan itself. There were indeed divergent opinions among US officials, but Chiang Kai-shek prevailed to the extent that US President Roosevelt appointed a special envoy to China favourable to Chongqing in the person of Patrick Hurley.

The overtly critical General Joseph Warren 'Vinegar Joe' Stilwell repeatedly clashed with Chiang over the Allied prosecution of the Burma campaign. In the China–Burma–India (CBI) theatre, Chiang was operational commander of the Chinese theatre, while the British controlled Burma and India. Stilwell's role in the CBI was that of a geographical administrative commander, on the same level as the commands of Dwight D. Eisenhower and Douglas MacArthur. Technically, Stilwell was therefore overall commander of Chinese troops. The general's plan to introduce reform into the Chinese army irked Chiang, who was fearful of such moves upsetting the delicate balance of political and military alliances in China that kept him firmly in power. Stilwell became extremely concerned about what he saw as Chiang's misappropriation of US lend-lease supplies to China. Increasingly, Chiang countermanded Stilwell's orders to his troops, accusing the US general of "recklessness, insubordination, contempt and arrogance".

Generalissimo and Madame Chiang Kai-shek with Lieutenant General Joseph W. Stilwell. (Photo US Army)

The launch by the Japanese of Operation Ichi-Go in April 1944 against the National Revolutionary Army, would see the antagonism between the head-strong Stilwell and Chiang boil over to an extent that would directly threaten Chiang's marriage with Washington. The polarization in interpretation of the strategic worth of Kweilin (Guilin) and the defence of Kunming resulted in Stilwell appealing to Roosevelt to intervene in the dispute with Chiang, of whom he wrote in his diary: "Crazy little bastard with that hickory nut he uses for a head ... usual cockeyed reasons and idiotic tactical and strategic conceptions. He is impossible!"

Suffice to say, the ailing US leader gave his general his unreserved support, writing to Chiang: "I have urged time and again in recent months that you take drastic action to resist the disaster which has been moving closer to China and to you. Now, when you have not yet placed General Stilwell in command of all

Enemy Offensive in China

Big Offensive Begun in Hunan

The long expected Japanese offensive in Hunan, along the Canton–Hankow railway south of Hankow, has begun (states Reuter from Chungking [Chongqing]). Supporting a Japanese drive southwards along the railway, another column east of the railway is moving along the highway via Tsungyang and Tungcheng, while yet another west of the railway is advancing in the Tungting Lake region, north-west of Changsha, via Hwajaung.

The importance of the new Japanese campaign cannot be minimised. Hunan is undoubtedly the richest province in Free China, producing more rice than even Szechuan, and is an important communications route between China's hinterland and East, as well as South-East China. Hunan Province is vital for raw materials—coal, iron, tungsten, tobacco, tea.

The Chinese have long anticipated this drive, and General Hsueh Yo, known as "Little Tiger," and his crack troops have valuable experience of four previous campaigns. The coming battle for Changhsa promises to be the biggest Chinese–Japanese clash since the battle for Hankow in 1938.

The Scotsman, Monday, 29 May 1944

forces in China, we are faced with the loss of a critical area ... with possible catastrophic consequences ... at once [place Stilwell] in unrestricted command of all your forces." Roosevelt ended by threatening to end all American aid if Chiang did not comply with the ultimatum.

Much to special envoy Hurley's chagrin, an ebullient Stilwell personally handed the executive letter to Chiang: "'I handed this bundle of paprika to the Peanut and then sank back with a sigh. The harpoon hit the little bugger right in the solar plexus and went right through him. It was a clean hit, but beyond turning green and losing his powers of speech, he did not bat an eye."

Responding to the "greatest humiliation I have been subjected to in my life", Chiang pointed an accusing finger at Roosevelt stating it was "all too obvious that the United States intends to intervene in China's internal affairs". Hurley stepped in once more, informing Washington that Stilwell was "incapable of understanding or co-operating with Chiang Kai-shek". That October, General Albert C. Wedemeyer replaced Stilwell in China.

The Japanese surrender took the Allies by surprise, for it had generally been assumed that a costly struggle still lay ahead, both against imperial Japanese forces on the mainland and then the taking of Japan itself. It had been believed that the great citadel of Japanese might on the continent was Manchuria, garrisoned by the redoubtable Kwantung Army. It seemed logical, therefore, to invite Stalin to participate in the Far Eastern War: with Nazi Germany collapsing in Europe, Moscow was persuaded to see the advantages of such a move.

Naturally, there would be a price tag attached to Soviet assistance. It therefore did not seem incongruous when Stalin, for example, claimed for his nation "former rights violated by the treacherous attack of Japan in 1904". At Yalta in February 1945, Roosevelt and Churchill readily and without reservation acceded to the Soviet conditions.

However, many of the 'rights' demanded concerned Chinese territory. This included Russia's right to reacquire the lease of Dairen and Port Arthur as naval bases, while the two principal railways of Manchuria would be operated by a joint Sino-Soviet company, taking cognizance of the "pre-eminent interests of the Soviet Union". Added to this was the contentious issue of Outer Mongolia.

Soviet Pacific Fleet marines hoisting the standard in Port Arthur, October 1945. (Photo RIA Novosti)

With the demise of the he ethnic-Manchu rulers of China's Qing Dynasty in 1911–12, this portion of the empire had claimed its independence. Then after the 1917 Russian Revolution, a Mongolian People's Republic had been established under Moscow's wing, but successive Chinese governments continued to assert their historic ownership of the 'Land of the Eternal Blue Sky', Mongolia. For the Soviets to join the alliance against Japan, Stalin dictated that China had to forsake this claim once and for all and formally ratify the independence of Outer Mongolia.

China was purposefully excluded from these tripartite deliberations, as Stalin needed a post-European war period of taking stock before taking on Japan, plus, the three leaders deemed it essential to keep their intentions strictly to themselves. At the right time, it would be incumbent on America and Britain to ensure Chinese acceptance of Stalin's conditions. On 14 August 1945, only days after Stalin had declared war on Japan, a Chinese delegation arrived in Moscow where they signed a treaty of "friendship and alliance", which, without China's knowledge, already embodied Stalin's prerequisites unilaterally agreed to by her Western allies on her behalf.

The manner and content of this transaction alone were sufficient to shatter the myth of China's status as a great power. The forfeiture of her claim to Outer Mongolia was especially difficult for all China's political structures and

Mao and Stalin postage stamp celebrating Sino-Soviet relations.

ideologies to stomach, regardless of their position on the nationalist spectrum. It is worth noting that the Nationalist regime on Formosa went on to repudiate the treaty, and again resuscitate China's inalienable right to sovereignty. Peiping, on the other hand—although the communists had been the most vocal antagonists of Mongolian secession—had acquiesced in the agreement, however distasteful they found it.

Even before the end of 1944, it was envisaged that Russian intervention in the war against Japan would be inevitable. To satisfactorily neutralize the massive Japanese garrison in Manchuria, the Soviet Red Army would march from Siberia and through Manchuria, where it would merge with Chinese Communist forces in northern China. A political settlement of the Communist–Nationalist dispute would, however, be essential.

Fully aware that a Soviet alliance in the Far East would greatly assist America in its prosecution of the Pacific War, Washington identified the imperative to bring Mao Zedong and Chiang Kai-shek into one mutually compatible government to avoid what might well become a fatal division of China. Mao's stand was simple and straightforward: Kuomintang one-party rule had to be dismantled in favour of a genuine national government of all "democratic" parties, including the communists. To such a coalition government, it would be possible to entrust the supreme command of the Red Army, but certainly not to the Chongqing regime in its present form.

However, to the Western Allies, for whom Mao's suggestion made total sense, there was a degree of resentment over Chiang Kai-shek's blatant lack of enthusiasm for the idea. All he was prepared to concede was to permit some low-level representation of communists and others in his government. He would be prepared to consider recommendations of a joint commission, including a communist and an American officer with regard to supplies for the Red Army, but with the strict proviso that the communists and their forces pledge loyalty to what would still be a Kuomintang-run regime. There was no compromise and the issues remained at stalemate until the end of the war.

During the evening of 10 August 1945, news of the Japanese offer to surrender reached both Yenan and Chongqing. At midnight, commander-in-chief of the Red Army, Chu Teh ordered his troops to commence disarming neighbouring Japanese garrisons in towns and along lines of communication, and to attack and eliminate any Japanese troops who resisted. The very next morning, Chiang Kai-shek countermanded the order, ordering all communist troops to

The cover of the 1 September 1937 *Asahigraph* magazine, depicting the Japanese Imperial Army marching through the Chaoyangmen Gate into Beijing.

remain where they were and under no circumstances should any move be made to disarm the Japanese. However, two days later, in a direct and ominous clash of purpose, Chu formally repudiated Chiang's orders as being prejudicial to national interests. The stand-off presented the first significant post-war crisis, which would have far-reaching ramifications. If the Japanese were to surrender to whatever Chinese forces were closest and capable, then almost all the occupied cities between the Great Wall and the Yangtse River would pass into communist hands.

Ignoring Chiang's attempts at ringfencing the communist forces, on 15 August Chu sent a message to the Japanese commanderin-chief in China, General Yasuji Okamura, advising him of the names of regional communist commissioners empowered to accept the surrender of Japanese troops, including representatives not merely from northern and central China, but also from the so-called 'liberated area' in the extreme south.

Japanese soldiers in China south of the Great Wall numbered 1,050,000 with 300,000 stationed in northern China, centred on Peiping, 350,000 at Hankow, 300,000 around Shanghai, and 100,000 in the area of Canton.

After a few days' considering his options, on 20 August General Okamura— the first officer in the Japanese army who instituted forced prostitution known as 'comfort women'—communicated his decision to his regional forces. Electing to rather have his fate determined by Chongqing, he instructed his forces to assist the Nationalist government in its mammoth task of reconstruction. Of significance, was his order for his troops to vigorously retaliate against any anti-Japanese activity by the communists. A week later, after some preliminary groundwork, a Nationalist high-command mission flew to Nanking where face-to-face discussions with General Okamura were initiated.

There was never any question that in Manchuria it would be the Russians who accepted the Japanese surrender. As it transpired, the dejected Kwantung Army, feeling betrayed by the sudden turn of events and weakened by the deployment of most of its battle-hardened troops to the Pacific theatre, had offered little in the way of resistance in the remaining days before surrender.

The puppet state of Manchuria had thus ceased to exist in the fourteenth year of its existence, and its titular ruler, Henry Pu Yi, who as a child had been installed as the final Manchu emperor of China, was carted off as a prisoner by the Soviets to Siberia. In 1950, he was repatriated to China for 're-education' as a citizen of the People's Republic. At first, it appeared that these events were

Surrender in Woodman's Hut

The surrender of the Japanese Kwantung Army in Manchuria was agreed in a woodman's hut near the frontier—the headquarters of Marshal Meretskov, Soviet commander of the First Far Eastern Front, Moscow radio reported to-day.

The Third Japanese Army began an organised capitulation immediately and was followed by the Fifth. Fifty-five thousand Japanese officers and men surrendered on the first day.

Russians in Daren and Port Arthur

Soviet airborne troops landed in Daren [sic] and Port Arthur and have begun disarming the garrisons, last night's Soviet communiqué stated.

The Japanese News Agency reported to-day: "The Soviet and Outer Mongolian forces are still on the offensive despite the willingness of the Japanese to comply immediately with the Allied demand for disarmament.

"The enemy seems to be attempting the invasion of the Mengchiang [Japanese Mongolian puppet state] and the Peking-Tientsin district."

Coventry Evening Telegraph, Thursday, 23 August 1945

the anticipated and inevitable outcome of Soviet intervention in the region, but it now began disturbingly ominous that Moscow had only just whet its appetite for adventurous expansionism farther south of its Oriental sojourn. Combined Soviet and Outer Mongolian forces went on to occupy Kalgan on the Great Wall, their armoured units probing some distance into Hopei Province in the direction of Peiping. Concurrently, the Japanese garrison in Inner Mongolia retired southward.

Through this all, Washington's fidelity to Chiang remained robust. It had become clear that the Nationalist leader would only be able to retake his old capital of Nanking with the provision of transport on an enormous logistical scale by the Americans. On 5 September, US aircraft commenced an airlift of Nationalist troops to the city, where, on 9 September, in a formal ceremony, the Japanese commander-in-chief handed over the instruments of surrender.

US General Douglas MacArthur reads the surrender terms to the Japanese representatives on board USS *Missouri* in Tokyo Bay, 2 September 1945. (US Army)

On 7 September 1945, a similar operation had started at Shanghai, while farther to the north, US troops landed by sea to disarm the Japanese. The Americans assumed the role of maintenance of public order at Tientsin on 1 October, while awaiting the arrival of the first Nationalist troops in the city on 21 October. The Americans immediately reopened the coastal railway which ran north from Tientsin (Tianjin) to Shanhaikwan (Shanhaiguan) where the Great Wall meets the sea.

Earlier, on 16 September, two US 7th Fleet warships entered the port of Tsingtao in Shantung, an arrangement made with Nationalist approval. There was vocal dissent from the communists, accusing Washington of effectively committing acts of hostility against the liberated areas. General Wedemeyer personally described the American translocation of Nationalist troops as "the greatest air and sea transportation in history". As a result, the Japanese were motivated to conform to General Okamura's directive and present a stronger front against the Communist guerrillas than they had against the Soviets at Kalgan. Armed clashes frequently took place, and it has been estimated that during the two months from the end of the war to the middle of October, about 1,500 Japanese had lost their lives in such engagements. Shansi Province provided the most striking example of Japanese–Chongqing collaboration, as it was here that Nationalist Governor Yen Hsi-shan decreed that the Japanese occupying force retain their weapons to participate in holding off the Communists.

However, the astute Mao Zedong had already formed his perception of the unprecedented circumstances which had ended the war against Imperial Japan in the Pacific theatre.

His views remaining unchanged; on 13 August 1945, Mao told a meeting of cadres held in Yenan that the atom bomb could not make Japan surrender, and that without the struggle waged by the people, atom bombs by themselves would not succeed. If atom bombs could end the war, then why was it necessary for the Allies to ask the Soviet Union to send its troops? Why did Japan not surrender when the two American atom bombs obliterated Hiroshima and Nagasaki? Why did she surrender the moment that Moscow sent in her troops? "The theory that weapons decide everything—the purely military viewpoint—all these are bourgeois influences in our ranks. We must constantly sweep these bourgeois things out of our ranks just as we sweep dust."

Notwithstanding Mao's Marxist rhetoric, and despite intransigent Nationalist governance, both Chinese and Western commentators still held out hope for a satisfactory resolution to the political impasse through reconciliation and compromise. On 28 August, Mao Zedong, accompanied by the US ambassador, arrived in Chongqing where, for the first time in twenty years, he engaged in direct dialogue with Chiang Kai-shek. Before leaving for the meeting, Mao, in discussion with his inner circle of followers, stated that he was willing to negotiate with some flexibility. For example, and in conformance with the fundamental philosophy of his Maoist strain of Marxist-Leninism, Mao advocated forsaking any strategies to gain control of the cities, and even reducing the size of the 'liberated areas'. Mao knew that both Moscow and the Western Allies feared the prospect of a civil war in China, so a show of moderation from him would encourage them to apply pressure on Chiang to momentarily step back to give the communist initiative a chance. The communists would know how to exploit such a pause to the best advantage.

Upon his arrival in Chongqing, Mao immediately called for national unity and a democratic government, conciliatory language which found favour among the general public, especially among students and intellectuals. In the talks

Above: A US-supplied Curtiss C-46D 'Commando' transport of the Chinese nationalist army.

Below: A former Japanese Kawasaki Ki-61 'Hien' fighter of the Chinese nationalist army.

themselves, all parties diligently maintained courteous interaction in a convivial atmosphere, and where the press captured the opposing Chinese leaders benevolently toasting the other's health. Mao was the perfect guest.

On 10 October, auspiciously a national holiday to mark the anniversary of the Revolution of 1911, it was announced that a provisional agreement had been signed by all parties. In a gesture of goodwill, Mao also dropped his original demand for a coalition. As a compromise, he had accepted a guarantee of the legality of all parties, the release of political prisoners, the disbanding of secret police, and the convening of a People's Consultative Conference. In return, he pledged that they, the Communists, under Chiang's direction, would do all in their power to avoid civil war, and that the Red Army would be reduced from forty to twenty divisions.

While the talks were in progress, however, the Communists persistently denounced what they perceived as the endless American intervention in the Nationalists' affairs. But the agreement of 10 October failed to even make it out the starting blocks.

Despite Mao's generous concessions, the communists were adamant that they were going to retain an independent military establishment—this was not on the negotiating table. As time went by, the inevitable implosion of the Kuomintang would find Mao waiting and ready to take control of China. Chiang's suspicions and distrust of the communists did not convince him that Mao's intentions were honourable. At the conference table Chiang may also have acted out the motions of entering into a peace pact with his adversary, but in the field his troops were ordered to intensify their attacks on the communists. And ultimately, Washington's support for their Chinese protégé did not waver, despite having encouraged Chiang to also show willing in the peace deliberations.

From the very first act of Soviet intervention in the region, the Chinese Communists had zealously proclaimed their solidarity with their Marxist-Leninist brothers from the north. Whilst guerrilla forces, described by their enemies as 'bandits', had been instrumental in the seizure of Kalgan, it was in their attacks against the Japanese in Manchuria itself that the communists seized the opportunity of proving their loyalty to Moscow.

The Russians, however, were largely ambivalent toward these would-be collaborators. The Kremlin's immediate objective was the establishment of Russian bases at Port Arthur and Dairen, so they were wary of being seen do be doing anything that might raise the alarm in Washington and potentially scupper their designs on these two east coast ports. Conversely, it was difficult

Above: The revolutionary army attacks Nanking, 1911.

Below: Rand McNally's map of East Asia, 1930s.

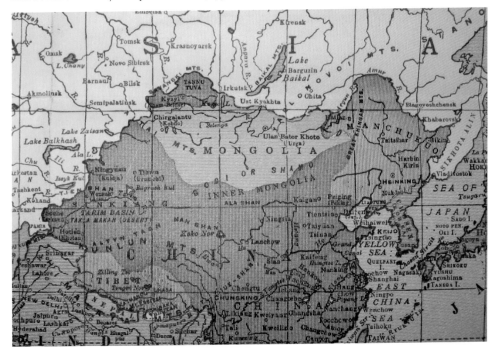

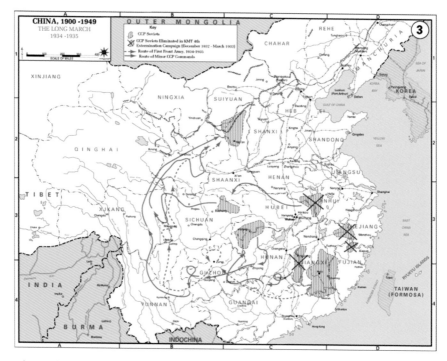

Above: The Long March, 1934–35. (Image US Army)

Below: Communist offensives, April–October 1949. (Image US Army)

The cover of the Japanese pictorial weekly magazine, *Asahigraph*, vol. 31 No. 1, 1938.

Left: A 1964 poster study of the 'Three Old Articles' by The [In-]House New Year's Picture Creative Group, Shanghai People's Fine Art Press. (via Thomas Fisher Rare Book Library)

Below: Eighth Route Army in Shanxi.

"American Invaders will be Defeated!" This posters depicts two PLA soldiers, each holding a book saying, respectively: "Soviet Army Defeated 12 million German Nazi, Italian , Japanese and other countries' soldiers during World War II" and "Chinese People's Liberation Army defeated 8 million soldiers of American Imperialist-sponsored Chiang Kai-shek's army". The bottom section shows defeated American capitalists in total disarray. (via Jason Ford)

Chairman Mao Zedong.

Generalissimo Chiang Kai-shek.

Above: Republic of China military parade, Taiwan. (Photo Batiste Pannetier)

Below: PLA navy guard of honour. (Photo Donna Miles)

Above: A PLA ZBD-04 infantry fighting vehicle, during China's 60th anniversary military parade. (Photo Dan in Beijing)

Below: Military parade commemorating the 70th anniversary of the end of the Second World War. (Photo Kremlin.ru)

Above: PLA air force Chengdu J-20 stealth, fifth-generation fighter. (Photo Art5)

Below: PLA army, air force and navy on parade, commemorating the 70th anniversary of the end of the Second World War.

Civil War in China

An undeclared civil war between Chinese Government troops and Chinese Communists is going on in Shantung [Shandong], the rich province which was the birthplace of Confucius and the cradle of Chinese civilisation, according to General Ho Shu Yaun, Governor of the province.

General Ho stated in Chungking yesterday that Communists control two-thirds of the 69,000 square miles of the province, and half its 38,000,000 people. He expressed the hope that the unity talks between Communist and Central Government leaders in Chungking would make it unnecessary for the Government to declare war on the Communists, but said that otherwise the Government troops would certainly have to fight for every square yard in Communist hands.

"I have come Chungking to stop this civil war," he said.

Opposing 100,000
General Ho declared that in every instance his troops had been attacked and forced to defend themselves, and put the strength of the Communist troops at 100,000. The Communists claim to have 110,000 troops and 90,000 regulars.

The Central Government had reduced its forces from 200,000 last year to 140,000. There are still some 80,000 Japanese troops in Shantung.

Bought From Japs!
Both the Communists and Government troops have been buying ammunition from the Japanese since 1939, the General disclosed. Silk and cotton has changed hands as well.

"After 1939 the morale of the Japanese Army began to decline very steeply. We bought freely from commanders of units who lined their own pockets. They simply told the higher ups that they had used more ammunition than they actually had."—Reuter.

Newcastle Journal, Tuesday, 23 October 1945

to reject the enthusiastic assistance proffered by the Chinese Communists, as they, the Soviets, were not in a position to object as strenuously as the Nationalists might have done to the widespread pillaging of Manchurian industrial installations, an activity almost equal in importance to the of the two ports.

The result was that nationalist troops arriving off southern Manchuria in American ships discovered, to their dismay that Mao's troops were already on station. They were refused permission to disembark. Special envoy General Wedemeyer, fully aware of the dangers, tried to dissuade Chiang from undertaking such a perilous military expedition to reclaim Manchuria. However, Chiang refused to take heed of Wedemeyer's advice, and once more the US acquiesced and shipped an invading nationalist army to the port of Chinwangtao, just within the Great Wall. In mid-November, Chiang's force struck northward.

A National Revolutionary Army soldier, armed with a Type-24 rifle, guarding US Air Force Curtiss P-40 Warhawk fighters. (Photo USAAF)

For the hapless Chiang, and despite early successes, the badly misjudged expedition would not only be an abject failure, but also his personal ruination and that of the KMT in mainland China; operating from their base in northern Manchuria, in 1948 the communists launched the great offensive that resulted in the expulsion of Chiang to the island of Formosa (Taiwan).

As 1945 drew to a close, however, no such calamitous thoughts had entered Chiang's mind. However, public opinion started showing signs of concern at the seemingly inevitable prospect of major bloodshed. In November, a league against civil war was formed in Chongqing itself, while in Kunming, 30,000 students took to the streets to protest against Chiang's course of action. The Americans also started to get nervous, so appointed one of her most distinguished Second World War soldiers, General George Marshall, as special envoy to China to replace Hurley, who had retired. His mission was simple but daunting: resuscitate the 10 October accord.

There was a tangible lessening of tension early in the new year, and by 10 January 1946, Marshall had somehow managed to get the parties back together for the signing of a ceasefire. With Zhou Enlai representing the communists, on the same day an all-party People's Consultative Conference, in accordance with the 10 October agreement, began a three-week session. The conference resolved that a national assembly would meet in May to draft a constitution and that the government should be administered by a State Council, of which not more than half should be Nationalists. In spite of the apparent resolution of the civil war issues, Chiang did not change the course of his master plan for a nationalist republic arising out of a communist defeat. He believed he had now created the subterfuge he desired: wartime refugees were streaming back to the occupied provinces where Chiang's name was held in high esteem and the Americans lauded as liberators from Shanghai to Peiping.

There was, however, no common ground between the two principal parties. Many would argue that, especially for Chiang, personal ambitions had clouded the ideological rationale for the ongoing civil war.

Before the end of 1946, the civil war was once more dominating life in China. Thoroughly disillusioned, General Marshall was packing his bags to return home. The situation for the populations of northern and eastern China was, in many ways, worse than it had been under the Japanese. The returning post-war refugees spoke openly about the growing incompetence of the Kuomintang. They related

Chiang Kai-shek, seated in a black coat, on a naval vessel, 1946.

the fact that American troops were leaving, with some remaining as advisers in the poisoned atmosphere of Chongqing.

In the second half of 1946, when the KMT national government announced the establishment of the Northeast Field Headquarters and dispatched more than 100,000 troops into Manchuria, the Soviet Union felt that her border was being threatened. As a consequence, they helped the Chinese Communists in their fight against the government troops. The central government might have prevented this if it had been genuinely interested in future peace.

The communists, however, knew that China was not yet ripe for socialism, thus they could only appeal to the KMT to allow them to participate in government affairs by forming a united government.

The situation in Manchuria had its own peculiarities. In 1931, the Northeast People's Revolutionary Red Army was organized in the Liao Tung and Sungari River areas, where it was commanded by Yang Ching-yd, Chao Hsiang-chih, Li Yen-lu and Chou Pao-chung. This army had fought against the Japanese until 1935, when it was united with other parties to form the Northeast United Army. This was followed in 1941 by Li Yun-ch'ang setting up the three military sectors of Hopei, Jehol and Liaoning. In July 1945, Lin Piao, Lu Cheng-ts'ao, Chang Hsueh,

Hsiao K'e and Zan I merged with the local commanders mentioned above to form the Northeast Democratic Army.

By early 1947, the communists had more than 300,000 regular troops in Manchuria. They were well equipped and supplied by the Soviet Union. Their strength was enhanced by the added presence of 30,000 Korean volunteers and a significant number of former Kwantung Army troops.

The Manchurians resented the central government dividing Manchuria into nine provinces, and appointing individuals from the south to key military and political posts. The KMT's lack of popularity was further worsened by mistakes in their tax, food collection, and conscription policies, the corruption of officials, the poor conduct of the nationalist troops, and their condescending attitude of

Russia's Claims in Far East

The announcement by officials of the U.S. War and State Departments that America is to begin collecting reparations from Japan immediately "even without full agreement with Russia" marks the climax of a prolonged wrangle in the Allied Council for Japan (which represents Great Britain, the U.S.A., Russia, and China, in Tokio.)

The whole reparations issue has been held up by Russia's claims. These have never been precisely disclosed, though one report, not inherently improbable, is that they hark back to the border "incidents" between Russia and Japan in the early thirties. What must be emphasised is that Russia has already paid herself handsomely for her eight days war with Japan, which must have been a very cheap campaign, as her forces were on the spot and the Japanese had little fight left in them.

Take first the machinery removed from Manchuria. According to the final report of Mr. Edwin W. Pauley, U.S. official investigator, Russia has described as "war booty" £171,600,000 worth of machinery and £600,000 worth of gold bullion. All the booty was taken between mid-September and early November 1945. The Soviet technical commission in charge was well planned and knew exactly what it wanted. The Russians were particularly keen on electrical equipment, and this "crippled practically all other industries and did more to break down the general economy than anything else."

After the Russians, the Chinese Communists took their toll, and then the mob stripped the factories of all woodwork, doors, and floors, and window frames. Mr. Pauley estimates that replacement costs will not be less than £400,000,000.

But "war booty" in Manchuria is almost trivial compared with Russia's territorial gains in the Far East, direct and indirect ... the southern half of the island of Sakhalein (of great mineral wealth) ... the long chain of Kurile islands ... North Korea ... Outer Mongolia ... and finally, in Manchuria, Russia still holds firmly to the ports of Dairen and Port Arthur. The Russo-Chinese Treaty of August 1945 also gave Russia joint control of the Chinese Eastern Railway, which connects Siberia and Vladivostok and runs down through Manchuria to Dairen and Port Arthur.

The Scotsman, Tuesday, 14 January 1947

A Japanese Type-97 'Chi-Ha' tank, Beijing military museum.

being superior to the local people. Manchuria was being treated as a conquered territory, leaving its population to feel that the communists were no good, and the Kuomintang was just about as bad. As the KMT and communists continued to fight each other in the territory—seemingly regardless of the local populace—there was a growing concern in Washington and Moscow that the Manchurians might resort to a "democratic revolution".

Political and military analysts in Washington believed that continued US support generated within the KMT a false sense of confidence to defeat the now enormous numbers of communist troops in Manchuria. Would the withdrawal of American aid result in a de-escalation of hostilities in the territory?

On 19 February 1947, the US Central Intelligence Group (the CIA was formed that September) produced an intelligence report on the Manchurian situation, offering a tranche of options:

Solutions

a. There is only one solution to the problem: to let a man who represents the ideas of the Manchurian people form a democratic, united, all-party government. Then, have a fair general election. At the same time, both Communist and Kuomintang troops should withdraw from Manchuria.

b. If there were a non-party government in Manchuria, the Soviets would not feel that their borders are being threatened. They would then turn to the reconstruction of their own country.

c. The Kuomintang did not appoint any Mongolians to positions of importance in Manchuria, and the East Mongols therefore set up their Autonomous Government. They would, however, join in the formation of a united government.

d. The only excuse the Communists have for being in Manchuria is to fight one-party dictatorship. A united government under a non-party leader would satisfy their demands.

The New Leader

The head of this new government should be a man praised by all people of Manchuria, a non-party man who has not had much to do with the Kuomintang, one known to all parties, one of international renown. He should also be known to the Russians and Inner-Mongolians; and a mediator between the Communists and the Kuomintang.

Kwantung Army generals.

General Ma Chan-shan

The only man besides Chang Hsueh-liang possessing the above-mentioned qual-
ifications is Ma Chan-shan. He began fighting the Japanese in Heilungchiang
Province in 1931, became internationally known as a hero, and is consequently
admired by all Manchurians.   He has never held membership in any party.

After he was defeated in Manchuria in 1932 he escaped through Russia and
Europe to China, met and became friendly with many Soviet leaders. He also
was stationed in Mongolia for several years, and the Mongols have a very good
impression of him. Although he himself left Heilungchiang Province in 1932,
most of his troops hid in forest areas and continued to fight the Japanese. After
1937, Ma was in contact with these troops, and his agents travelled back and
forth over Manchuria. He now has about 150,000 men in Kirin, Heilungchiang,
Liaoning and Jehol Provinces. He is respected by the Kuomintang, and at the
same time he is praised by the Communists as a non-party man and a national
hero of China.

4. FOR THE PEOPLE BY THE PEOPLE

The People's Liberation Army (PLA) traces its roots to the Nanchang Uprising of 1 August 1927. Nanchang, a large town 400 miles inland from Shanghai, had already been the site a mutiny by several thousand Cantonese troops in February that year, in which some of their officers were killed and the town looted.

The growing left–right rift in the Kuomintang ultimately resulted in the acrimonious dissolution of the first Kuomintang–Communist Party of China alliance. On 1 August, in Nanchang, communist commanders of the garrison, including Zhu De, He Long and Zhou Enlai, led 20,000 troops in rebellion and seized control of the town.

Escaping the siege imposed by the Nationalist army, the rebels fled to the Jinggang Mountains on the border between Hunan and Jiangxi provinces, where they joined forces with Mao Zedong. The 34-year-old future iconic leader of Communist China, was also a fugitive after having staged a failed insurrection against the Kuomintang and the landlords of Hunan early in September—the Autumn Harvest Uprising. In this, the first armed resistance by the communists, Mao had led a small rural peasant army, an event that planted the seed for Mao's vision of a rural-based guerrilla war.

The combined forces, under the leadership of Mao and Zhu, comprised an amorphous 'army' of communists, bandits, Nationalist deserters and destitute peasants. This embryo of the People's Liberation Army was titled the First Workers' and Peasants' Army, or Red Army, the military wing of the CCP.

Employing guerrilla tactics, for which Mao Zedong would become globally renowned as the founder of a revolutionary military strategy, the Red Army would survive numerous cordon and sweep campaigns by superior KMT forces. During the Fifth Encirclement Campaign against Jiangxi Soviet from September 1933 to October the following year, Chiang Kai-shek, in his role as commander-in-chief of Kuomintang forces, and assisted by his German advisers Hans von Seeckt and Alexander von Falkenhausen and local warlords, neutralized the communist control of the soviet. Red Army casualties were massive, and, by September 1934, the towns and cities towns of Ruining, Huichang, Xingguo, Ningdu, Shicheng, Ninghua and Changting were all that remained of the Chinese soviet republic.

Terrorism in China

Communists Whipped and Executed

Ningpo, Friday: The Nationalist General, Yang Hu, commanding the Shanghai area, who recently arrived here with a bodyguard of 200 men and 12 executioners, with a view to dealing with local Communists, has so far executed at least three. The unfortunate victims were first subjected to a whipping with bamboo for the purpose of extracting information.

The first case was that of a young school teacher, who, after fifty strokes with a "big bamboo," broke down and confessed the names of his alleged confederates, many of whom were arrested.

Secondly, a post office employee, head of a local labour union, was severely beaten, but no information was extracted from him. He then suffered beheading without whimpering.

The third victim was a woman Communist, who, after being terribly beaten till her back was one mass of blood, was led before a firing squad and shot.

The Chinese here are horrified, and say that actions such as these must undoubtedly react against General Chiang Kai-shek, head of the Nanking Government, and General Yang Hu's superior.—Reuter.

Northern Whig, Saturday, 2 July 1927

At this critical juncture, and with internal politics in the CCP rising to the fore, the Red Army temporarily abandoned its guerrilla tactics, withdrew from Jiangxi, and commenced what became the epic Long March of 1934–35. The peasant-worker-soldier philosophy enshrined in Mao's army was tempered during the Long March, providing a legendary and potent symbol of the indispensable role of the Red Army in the people's revolution, a legacy inherited in perpetuity by its successor, the People's Liberation Army (PLA). The rigours of the experience significantly enhanced Mao's political power and conclusively proved the value of his strategy of guerrilla warfare to the party and the Red Army.

The divisions of the Chinese Workers' and Peasants' Red Army were titled according to random historical circumstances. Early communist units formed by troops defecting from Kuomintang forces, tended to keep their original designations.

Nationalist Eighth Route Army cheering at the Great Wall, Liaoyuan, Hebei, 1937.

However, this unstructured titling of scattered communist-controlled areas during the civil war, made central control extremely problematic.

By the time of the Long March in October 1934, many of these diverse units had been amalgamated into three groups: the First Front Red Army (Hong Yi Fangmian Jun), the Second Front Red Army (Hong Er Fangmian Jun) and the Fourth Front Red Army (Hong Si Fangmian Jun).

The First Front Red Army, raised from the First, Third and Fifth Red armies in southern Jiangxi, was commanded by Bo Gu and Li De; the Fourth Front Red Army, led by Zhang Guotao was raised from several smaller units in the Szechuan–Shensi border region. Subsequently, the Second Front Red Army, commanded by He Long and Jen Pi-shih, was formed in eastern Kweichow by the unification of the Second and Sixth Red armies. A Third Front Red Army was never formed, and the three armies retained their historical titles of First, Second and Fourth Front Red armies until the communist forces were nominally

September 1937 *Asahigraph* magazine image depicting a group of Japanese soldiers shouting "*Banzai!*" in Nankou, Beijing.

integrated into the National Revolutionary Army, which resulted in the emergence of the Eighth Route Army and the New Fourth Army during the Second Sino-Japanese War.

In 1937, the Red Army joined up with the KMT to form a second united front with against the Japanese army, but this was only an ostensible display of cooperation with the KMT against a common invasive enemy. On the ground, however, the CCP was using the Red Army to expand its influence while spearheading resistance against the Japanese in northern China. At the time of the conflict, the Red Army's strength stood at one million, with a militia force of two million in support. Conventional-war engagements by the Red Army against the Japanese and KMT troops were not common, as guerrilla tactics were the preferred mode of warfare.

The Red Army's experiences of the late 1930s and early 1940s further nurtured Mao's thinking of armed struggle, ultimately resulting in his development of the concept of the 'people's war'—the mantra of the Red Army and its successor, the People's Liberation Army.

> ## Huge Rewards for Killing Communists
>
> Planes Drop Leaflets in Red Province of China
>
> A fleet of Government aeroplanes has flown over the Communist areas of Kiang-Si Province, China, and dropped 100,000 leaflets offering rewards for the capture of various "Red" leaders dead or alive.
>
> The value of two of them, Chu Teh and Mao Tse-Tung, is assessed at £6,250 each; £5,000 is offered for the capture of five others; while £3,750 will be paid for their heads.
>
> A reward of £1,875 will be given for the capture of any "Red" army commander, and £1,250 for their heads.
>
> *Nottingham Evening Post*, Monday, 20 November 1933

Mao was further influenced in this doctrine by the writings of fourth century BC Chinese military strategist Sun Zi, Soviet and other theorists and the folklore of peasant uprisings found in stories such as in the classical novel *Shuihu Zhuan* (Water Margin) and the stories of the Taiping Rebellion.

In this manner, Mao created an all-encompassing politico-military doctrine for the waging of a revolutionary war. By the very nature of the prescribed means to stage a revolution, Mao's 'People's War' constituted political, economic, and psychological measures as integral to military struggle against a superior enemy. The success of a people's war relied entirely on the mobilization of the populace in support of conventional and guerrilla forces, in a manner that would produce optimum motivation to balance out the inadequacy of weaponry and technology inferior to that of the foe. There would be three progressive stages to a protracted struggle: strategic defence, stalemate and offense.

During the first phase, enemy forces were drawn into one's own familiar surrounds to overextend, dissipate and isolate them. The Red Army would establish transient base areas from which to badger the enemy—these bases could easily be abandoned if threatened to preserve Red Army strength. In keeping with the integral role of the peasants in the revolution, Mao introduced 'Eight Points of Attention', standing orders for the Red Army, enjoining his troops to respect the peasants and not to harm them in any way, even if the soldiers were in need of

Nationalist Eighth Route Army in action, at Futuyu, Great Wall, 1938.

food and supplies. This policy won massive popular support for Mao and the communists among the rural peasant populations.

The second phase was a war of attrition in which superior numbers and morale were employed to tire the enemy in areas where guerrilla operations prevailed.

In the third and final phase, by which time a state of parity would have been achieved between the two opposing forces, the Red Army would switch to regular warfare and ultimately defeat the enemy.

The Chinese Civil War that followed Japan's capitulation at the end of the Second World War was characterized by Mao's revolutionary strategies. The Red Army, recently retitled the People's Liberation Army (PLA), again used the principles of waging a people's war: strategic withdrawal, wage a war of attrition, and then abandon cities and communication lines to the numerically greater Kuomintang forces.

In 1947, the PLA launched a counteroffensive during a short-lived strategic stalemate. By the summer of 1948, the communist forces entered the decisive strategic offensive stage using conventional warfare as the KMT forces fell back before rapidly disintegrating on the Chinese mainland in 1949. The following year, the PLA seized Hainan Island and Xizang.

In January 1949, the CCP Central Military Commission undertook a reorganization of the PLA regional armies into four field armies.

In northwestern China, Peng Dehuai was placed in command of the newly designated First Field Army. He would also serve as political commissar. The First Field Army consisted of the 1st and 2nd corps armies, with a strength of 134,000 men. After 1949, the First Field Army had control of the provinces of Shanxi, Gansu, Qinghai, Ningxia, and Xinjiang.

The Second Field Army assumed control of the PLA in central China, with Liu Bocheng in command, while future leader of China Deng Xiaoping was appointed political commissar. The Second Field Army comprised the 3rd, 4th and 5th armies, with a special technical column in support, and numbered 128,000 men. After 1949, this field army was redeployed to southwestern China where it took control of Yunnan, Guizhou, Sichuan, Xikang provinces and the future autonomous region of Tibet.

The Third Field Army commanded PLA forces in eastern China, under the command of Chen Yi. Comprising the 7th, 8th, 9th, and 10th corps armies and the

PLA generals, from left to right, Deng Xiaoping, He Long and Zhu De, 1949.

headquarters of the special technical troops, it had a strength of 580,000 men. After 1949, the Third Field Army remained on station on the east coast, controlling Shandong, Jiangsu, Zhejiang, Anhui and Fujian.

In Manchuria, PLA forces were designated the Fourth Field Army under Lin Biao. The army comprised the 12th, 13th, 14th, 15th corps armies, special technical troops, the Column of Guangdong and Guangxi, and the 50th and 51st corps.

With the founding of the People's Republic of China on 1 October 1949, the People's Liberation Army became a national armed force, a clumsy, five-million-strong, largely peasant army. By 1950, the PLA incorporated 10,000 in the air force (formed in 1949 and 60,000 in the navy (formed in 1950). At that time the demobilization of poorly trained or politically undesirable troops had begun, which saw the PLA streamlined to a strength of 2.8 million by 1953.

However, the PLA was essentially still only a mass of foot soldiers with limited mobility, logistics, ordnance and communications. Mao and the new leaders of China, in recognizing an urgent need to modernize the military, looked to the Soviet Union, and in February 1950, the signing of the Sino-Soviet Treaty of Friendship, Alliance and Mutual Assistance paved the way for Moscow to assist with modernization of the new communist nation's defence forces.

A US-made M3A3 Stuart tank of the PLA near the Yangtze River, 1949.

Arms for Chinese Reds: Soviets Accused

The Chinese National Government intends, it is understood, to accuse Russia of giving aid and arms to the Chinese Communist armies. In advising the British Government that they intend to raise the matter at the fourth session of the General Assembly of the United Nations, which opened in New York yesterday, the Chinese Government indicates that it will claim that, in making arms available to the Chinese Communists, Russia has violated the Russo-Chinese pact of friendship of August 1945. The U.S. Government, it is understood, has received similar notification from the Chinese National Government.

It seems probable (adds the Press Association Diplomatic Correspondent), that the British and the U.S. delegations to the Assembly will wait to see on what grounds the Chinese Government base their accusations before deciding their attitude towards it. But it is probable the main allegation will be that, after the end of the war against Japan, Russia saw to it that much captured Japanese equipment and arms fell into the hands of the Chinese Communists.

If the Chinese National Government proceed with their intention of bringing the matter to the attention of the General Assembly, then the whole question of the Chinese civil war may be debated.

Meanwhile the Communist forces in China continue their advances against the Nationalist armies.

Hartlepool Northern Daily Mail, Wednesday, 21 September 1949

The Korean War further highlighted the weaknesses of Chinese armed forces equipped with inferior technology. Known as the Chinese People's Volunteers, their sheer weight of numbers provided initial success in pushing back American-led United Nations troops and, even though this was the PLA's first baptism of modern firepower, they still managed to bring the UN forces to a stalemate.

However, the unsupported infantry sustained significant troop and matériel losses during their assaults on diverse and modern combined arms firepower. For China—and Moscow—the Korean combat experience confirmed PLA deficiencies, galvanizing Soviet assistance in equipping and reorganizing the Chinese forces.

5. RED VICTORIOUS

The US Central Intelligence Agency (CIA) *Historical Review Program,* ORE 45-48 of 22 July 1948, reported, with concern, on the rapidly deteriorating situation in civil-war-torn China in the first quarter of 1948.

Within Nationalist China, the power and status of Chiang Kai-shek had steadily weakened due to the unsuccessful prosecution of the civil war under his leadership, allied to his apparent unwillingness and inability to implement positive reforms in the Kuomintang. Opposition, both within the KMT and among dissident elements, centred mainly in Hong Kong, was gaining momentum. In addition, deteriorating economic conditions were having a detrimental cumulative impact on the political infrastructure of the national government. Added to this, the armed forces of the Chinese Communists had been able to seize the tactical initiative on an ever increasingly large scale. Even with existing levels of American assistance, it had become highly improbable that the Nationalist army could successfully defend all of its present territories much beyond the immediate future.

Since mid-1947, when the Nationalist army was forced on the defensive by Mao's forces, the advantage which the Nationalist army held over the communists in 1945–46 had been gradually reduced to the level of parity—true to Mao's doctrine—and in certain areas, both the initiative and advantage had swung to the Red Army. As the capabilities of the Nationalist army tumbled, the escalating military pressure of the communists in central, northern and northeastern China further eroded nationalist control of sectors in these regions.

As at 1 March 1948, the tactical troop strength in the Nationalist army was estimated to be around 2.2 million. These regular units were augmented by about 500,000 service troops and some 500,000 additional provincial troops of diverse combat capabilities. Added to these strengths, the nationalist ground forces were supplemented by a small navy and air force which, being unopposed, enjoyed a tactical and strategic advantage beyond their strengths. The entire nationalist military establishment, however, was afflicted by glaring structural and command shortcomings. Two and a half years of combat wear and tear had substantially reduced the proportion of combat-fit men in its tactical units, while fighting and inadequate maintenance had reduced the numbers and effectiveness of its

Republic of China soldiers servicing fighter.

Big Victories Claim

China Communists Report Capture of 17 Generals

The "North-Eastern People's Liberation Army" in Manchuria captured 17 Chinese Government generals in the three months ending March 1, according to a communiqué quoted by Tass, the official Soviet news agency, yesterday.

The report said that 105,000 Chinese Government troops were captured and 73,000 square miles, with a population of more than 6,000,000, occupied.

China's first elected National Assembly met in Nanking for the first time yesterday, with more than 100 "rebel" members of the Kuomintang (Government) Party held under "hotel arrest" and 100 others boycotting the session in sympathy. The "rebels" had refused to give up their seats under an arrangement with the opposition parties.

The Assembly heard Generalissimo Chiang Kai-shek denounce the Communists, and members swore to uphold the Constitution.

Western Morning News, Tuesday, 30 March 1948

arms and logistics. Furthermore, the Nationalist army had virtually depleted its combat reserve by unrealistically prolonged garrison commitments. Enlistment and conscription drives, the latter all too often characterized by brutal press-gang methods, had failed to secure the recruits necessary for meaningful field replacements. The adequate training of such recruits had been lacking and the leadership incompetent and corrupt.

One of the most serious deficiencies in the KMT military establishment was the absence of a well-structured, compiled and executed indoctrination programme to counter the powerful 'education' received by their armed opponents. There was also a very noticeable absence of empathy between officers and their troops. As a consequence, morale suffered badly, bordering on defeatism in areas where the communist threat was the greatest.

KMT intelligence had been found wanting—ineffective and often erroneous in the assessment of communist capabilities as well as intentions. The outcome was that the Nationalist army was regularly caught on the wrong foot, with the result that it often suffered serious losses that could have been avoided.

Weapons and equipment in the Nationalist army were noted for their lack of compatible uniformity, sourced as they were from a miscellany of European, American, and Chinese arsenals. It was largely because of their American matériel, which included air and naval weaponry, that the Nationalists enjoyed superior firepower. Whilst Chiang's forces had a slight advantage over the communists in terms of arsenal capacity, unmanageable, lengthy transportation lines, shortages of the whole range of transport vehicles, and constant and widespread communist guerrilla marauding in the northern areas had created profoundly complicated and virtually unsolvable logistic problems for the KMT. As a consequence, they routinely found their operational capabilities hamstrung by shortages of combat matériel at the fronts.

With initial advantages in numbers and firepower, the nationalists set about capturing the key cities of northern China and Manchuria and to open the main terrestrial lines of communications. In this, however, they failed badly. They went about employing conventional offensive tactics, but lacked adequate logistical support and competent leadership to pull it off. For the last twelve months of the war, they largely found themselves forced by the communists to adopt a defensive role, generally employing a system of static-defence strongholds, ensconcing themselves within prepared defensive structures while passively waiting for the communists to attack their secure position. With more modern arms and an air

PLA troops occupy the
presidential palace,
Peking, 1949.

force, the nationalists were able to concentrate their forces at strategically key
locations, e.g., Mukden, where they were successful in deterring the communists
from launching meaningful assaults on such fortified positions. By controlling
strategic railway junctions in this manner, the nationalists denied the communists access to vital traffic on these lines.

From March 1948, however, there was a discernible rethink in KMT strategic
concepts when they began to demonstrate a new disposition to evacuate points
"lacking in strategic importance". The old communist capital of Yanan, Kirin
(Jilin) in Manchuria, the majority of the coastal towns on the northern shore of
the Shandong peninsula, and Tolun in the Inner Mongolian province of Chahar
had already been abandoned. Prior to this, the nationalists had long refused to
contemplate even tactically productive withdrawals. Their readiness now to fall
back was largely attributable to an acceptance among national government leaders of very real limitations in resources.

Due to the KMT tactics generally following a network of static defences, the
communists were able to choose the time and place of attacking the enemy.
Occasionally, KMT leaders formulated plans for broad offensives, but since the
end of the Shantung Campaign in October 1947, nationalist action had been
restricted to local, relatively small-scale counteroffensives. As time progressed,
even the undertaking of such local actions would be gradually and progressively
curtailed.

By mid-1948, the Communist army had started metamorphosing itself from a guerrilla-style formation into a more orthodox military machine. From being a force fighting small-scale, hit-and-run battles against the superior government forces, it had now matured into being capable of taking the war to the KMT, engaging in actions over wide areas and over extended periods of time.

On 1 March 1948, the Communist army consisted of 1.15 million regulars that were periodically augmented by forces of irregulars pressed into active service as and when the local situation warranted it. Historically, the communists had been able to recruit new men—by persuasion or by force—as quickly as they are able to feed and equip them. Irregulars, on the other hand, provided trained personnel familiar with communist methodology. An increasing trend of defection from nationalist units also provided the communists with manpower of limited numbers and usefulness.

Communist morale had become tangibly superior to that of the nationalists as the result of a well-conceived and ongoing propaganda campaign. Officers in the communist forces were selected and promoted strictly upon field-tested merit, their leadership competent, honest and cordial with the troops.

The PLA enters Peking.

What Communism is for John Chinaman

Reliable observers estimate that more than half of China's four hundred million population are now under Communist control.

What sort of regime is this undoubtedly dynamic growth that has made such gains since the end of the war with Japan? At the present rate of increase it is not impossible that the Communists will be masters of China in the two years that they themselves predict. A dozen or more American writers have praised the Chinese Communists as knights without armour engaged in building a new world on the ruins of the old. One or two are avowed Communists who can see nothing wrong with their chosen party, but others are independent with no political axes to grind.

Here is the general picture of Red China as these witnesses described it to me:

Everybody agreed that America is the target of Communist hatred. The United States is the Enemy Number One of Communist China and is bitterly attacked in writing and speech. Soviet Russia is as frequently lauded.

Even the most bitter opponents of the Communists, including Catholic priests, agree in praising the regular troops of the Red Army, who are described as well-disciplined and bold fighters, who treat the Chinese peasantry well, unlike both their own militia and the great bulk of the Nationalist armies. Near the front their behaviour is worse than at the rear, whereas the reverse is the case with Communist officials, who conciliate newly-occupied areas and later put the screw on.

The Red troops are well clad, but not well armed. They are recruited on a quota basis, each Communist district being obliged to provide so many men according to its population, the decision as to who shall go being left to the villagers. Of the three rulers under which the Chinese have suffered—suffered is the word in the last ten years—the least unpopular was that of the Japanese. The Communists are thought to be worse that the Japanese and Chiang Kai-shek's Government worse than either.

Aberdeen Press and Journal, Tuesday, 2 March 1948

Arising out of their aggressive propaganda and land redistribution programmes, the communist forces had attracted substantial support from the poorer Chinese peasants, who not only helped feed and clothe the communist army, but also provided an almost endless source of replacements. Added to this, these peasants—the 'invisible eyes and ears'—provided extremely valuable local intelligence which enabled the communists to repeatedly launch surprise attacks on nationalist garrisons, to hit only weakly defended posts, and to ambush convoys of nationalist troops. The communists also employed an extensive fifth column, which provided key advance intelligence while engaging in political propaganda activities.

The weapons and equipment of the communist army were acquired primarily from Imperial Japanese Army stocks cached in Manchuria and northern China during and after the Second World War. From around 1947, the increasingly successful communists were able to supplement their weaponry by capturing large quantities of nationalist matériel, including equipment of US origin. Consequently, communist matériel now showed the same diversity as that of the nationalists. Mao's forces, however, restricted their actions to where logistical support was sound.

Mao's people's army.

Early in the civil war, the communists formulated a strategic pattern for prosecuting their struggle, based on a pragmatic appraisal and acceptance of their own limitations in manpower, weapons, technology and logistics. The strategy hinged on guerrilla tactics, which had allowed them to realize the optimum results with limited resources. The strategy, in its early phases, aimed at disrupting the KMT's efforts whenever and wherever possible: stealth hits on lines of communications, the isolation of entire active areas to prevent mutual support, and the encirclement of nationalist-controlled urban areas to stem the rural–urban flow of farm produce and raw materials.

As an integral adjunct of the guerrilla war of attrition, the communists would lure nationalist forces into extended, vulnerable salients, such as the vastness of Manchuria, and there isolate and neutralize smaller individual units. Mao refused to engage in pitched battles, unless they had accomplished a superiority in men and matériel to negate the superior nationalist firepower. Mao was insistent that his forces should not undertake any battle unless they outnumbered the enemy by having double, triple, quadruple, even five or six times that of the enemy strength. Whilst this strategy had ensured minimum casualties and the expansion of armed units, it also allowed the KMT to hold onto important cities situated in areas where the rural areas has been secured and subverted by the communists. Over time, the communists had therefore been able to gradually bolster their forces until they were strong enough to challenge the nationalists' tenure of even such urban centres.

Mao's strategic advantage was demonstrably extremely successful in Manchuria in the winter of 1948. The communist Northeast Field Army in the Liaoshen Campaign conducted a fourteen-week offensive that culminated on 30 October in the envelopment of Mukden (Shenyang)—the largest city in northeastern China—and destruction of seven nationalist divisions. The weakened nationalists, having already lost control of the countryside, had been unable to reopen the corridor along the railway from the Great Wall northward to the beleaguered Mukden.

With the capture of the rail junction at Suping and Kirin, the communists had gained control of the entire Manchurian rail network, except the junctions at Changchun and Mukden. Such possession and operation of these lines provided significantly enhanced logistic support, greater mobility, and, with it, far greater hitting power against the KMT.

Mao's military activity in northern and central China, however, had been more limited in strategy, in that it was more of a diversionary operation. Here, communist operations adhered to guerrilla tactics of rapid movement within a large area, all the while harassing nationalist communications, interspersed with occasional feints or fleeting attacks on key nationalist positions before retreating before the enemy could react. These tactics not only proved extremely disruptive to Chiang's forces, but also resulted in the nationalists having to commit disproportionately large numbers of troops to counter the communists' annoying activities. The nationalists were thus unable to release reserve units to reinforce other fronts without running the risk of losing control of the areas from where those troops had been withdrawn. An example of such a setback had in fact taken place in Shantung (Shandong) Province, where the gains of a nationalist offensive have been all but completely negated by the communists when regular nationalist divisions translocated to counter increasing communist actions in Manchuria and central China.

Communist military activity in vastly separate regions in northern, northwestern and central China kept the nationalists struggling and failing to find the main body of the elusive enemy, and unable to predict when and where the next communist threat would arise.

The telegram below, addressed to the Eastern China and Central Plains Field Armies and the Bureaus of the Central Committee of the Communist Party of

PLA troops during the Taiyuan Campaign, 1949.

China in those two areas, was written by Mao Zedong for the Revolutionary Military Commission of the Party's Central Committee.

The Huaihai campaign, or the Battle of Hsupeng, was one of the three campaigns (the other two were Liaoshen and Pingjin) of decisive significance in the Chinese People's War of Liberation. The campaign was fought by the combined forces of the Eastern China and Central Plains field armies and the regional troops of the eastern China and Central Plains areas. In the campaign, over 555,000 KMT troops were killed or captured. The structure of the campaign laid out by Mao, the communists went on to boast, was the reason for its rapid and complete success.

Here are a few points for your consideration concerning the dispositions for the Huai-Hai campaign.

1. In the first stage of this campaign, the central task is to concentrate forces to wipe out Huang Po-Tao's army, effect a breakthrough in the centre and capture Hsinanchen, the Grand Canal Railway Station, Tsaopachi, Yihsien, Tsaochuang, Lincheng, Hanchuang, Shuyang, Pihsien, Tancheng, Taierhchuang and Linyi.

   To achieve these objectives, you should use two columns to wipe out each enemy division, that is to say, use six or seven columns to cut up and wipe out the enemy's 25th, 63rd and 64th Divisions. Use five or six columns to hold off and attack enemy reinforcements. Use one or two columns to annihilate the one brigade under Li Mi at Lincheng and Hanchuang, and strive to capture those two towns in order to menace Hsuchow from the north so that the two armies under Chiu Ching-chuan and Li Mi will not dare move east in full strength as reinforcements. Use one column plus regional formation in southwestern Shantung to make a flank attack on the Hsuchow–Shangchiu section of the railway in order to tie down a portion of Chiu Ching-chuan's army (as three enemy divisions under Sun Yuan-liang are about to move east, it is hoped that Liu Po-cheng, Chen Yi and Teng Hsiao-ping will dispose their troops at once to attack the Chengchow-Hsuchow line and so tie down Sun Yuan-liang's army). Use one or two columns to operate in the Suchien–Suining–Lingpi area to hold down Li Mi's army.

   These dispositions mean that before the objective of annihilating the three divisions of Huang Po-tao's army can be achieved, more than half our total force has to be employed against the two armies under Chiu Ching-chuan and Li Mi to tie down, check and destroy part of them. The dispositions should, by and large, be similar to those of last September for capturing Tsinan and attacking the enemy's reinforcements; otherwise it will be impossible to achieve the objective of annihilating the three divisions of Huang Po-tao's army. You must strive to conclude the first stage two to three weeks after the start of the campaign.

2. In the second stage, use about five columns to attack and wipe out the enemy in Haichow, Hsinpu, Lienyunkang and Kuanyun and capture these towns. It is calculated that by then the enemy's 54th and 32nd Divisions will very likely have been transported by sea from Tsingtao to the Haichow–Hsinpu–Lienyunkang area.

   Altogether three enemy divisions will be in that area, including the one division already there; therefore we must use five columns to attack them and employ the remaining forces (our main strength) to tie down the two armies under Chiu Ching-chuan and Li Mi, again on the principle underlying the dispositions made in September for capturing Tsinan and attacking the enemy's reinforcements. You must strive to conclude this stage also in two to three weeks.

3. In the third stage, it may be assumed that the battle will be fought around Huaiyin and Huai-an. By that time the enemy will have increased his strength by about one division (the reorganized 8th Division in Yentai is being shipped south); therefore we must be prepared again to use about seven columns as the attacking force, while using the rest of our main force to strike at and hold down the enemy's reinforcements. This stage will also take about two to three weeks.

   These three stages will take about a month and a half to two months.

4. You are to complete the Huai-Hai campaign in two months, November and December. Rest and consolidate your forces next January. From March to July you will be fighting in co-ordination with Liu Po-cheng and Teng Hsiao-ping to drive the enemy to points along the Yangtse River, where he will dig in. By autumn your main force will probably be fighting to cross the Yangtse.

The Huaihai campaign was fought by the People's Liberation Army (PLA) over a large territory in Kiangsu, Shantung, Anhwei and Honan provinces, centring on Hsuchow, and extending as far as Haichow in the east, Shangchiu in the west, Lincheng (Hsuehcheng) in the north and the Huai River in the south.

The KMT forces concentrated in this theatre of war consisted of five armies and the troops of three 'Pacification Zones'. On the side of the PLA, more than 600,000 participated in the campaign, including sixteen columns from the Eastern China Field Army, seven columns from the Central Plains Field Army, and regional armed forces from the Eastern China Military Area, the Central Plains Military Area and the Hopei–Shantung–Honan Military Area.

Chiang Planes Bomb Mukden

An hour after Communist armies completed the occupation of the Manchurian capital, Mukden, General Chiang Kai-shek planes bombed the city, it was reported from Nanking last night. Chiang's Government has not yet confirmed the loss of Mukden, but has admitted "reverses" in Manchuria.

Communists claim to have cut the escape corridor south to the port of Yingkow, 115 miles from Mukden. Yingkow evidently remains in Chiang's hands. The cruiser Chungking (formerly the British cruiser Aurora), is reported on guard there. Only one Nationalist Army stands between North China and the Communists are now in complete control of Manchuria.

Their "Monty"
Commanded by General Fu Tso-yi, the "Montgomery of North China" and one of Chiang Kai-shek's most able commanders, it is the Nationalists' only hope if the Communists turn south.

Chiang's position is regarded as precarious. With five of his armies scattered by the Communists, he is also facing an economic storm. His Premier and Finance Minister resigned yesterday because of the collapse of the price-control policy.

Communist chances of controlling the whole of China were re-affirmed in Bucharest last night by Mao Tse-tung, President of the Chinese Communist Party, writing in the Cominform Bulletin. The Chinese Red Army, he wrote, now occupies 24.5 per cent of the entire National territory and 35.3 per cent of the population.

Daily Herald, Tuesday, 2 November 1948

The PLA offensive lasted sixty-five days, from 6 November 1948 to 10 January 1949, during which time the KMT saw the decimation of fifty-six of its divisions, including four divisions that had deserted to join the communists. A further two armies, commanded by Liu Ju-ming and Li Yen-nien—reinforcements from Nanking—were forced back. As a result of the campaign, those parts of the eastern China and Central Plains areas north of the Yangtze River were almost entirely liberated.

The course of the war was not what the West, or the KMT for that matter, expected. With support from Washington and veteran organizations, everyone expected a victory for the KMT over Mao. The nationalist armies, however, were shattered and demoralized from the long conflict with the Japanese occupiers. Consequently, the fresh and highly motivated PLA was able to score many victories over the KMT.

Mao addresses followers. (Photo US NARA)

By 1948, the crisis was looking bad for the nationalists, and favourable for the communists. When the Liaoshen Campaign ended on 2 November, the roles and fortunes of the PLA and the KMT's National Revolutionary Army had reversed. For the first time in the civil war, the PLA was stronger than the nationalists, an advantage on which the communists capitalized.

At this time, Mao's attention moved to central China, where communist strategist Su Yu was implementing his master plan. Earlier in the year, Su contemplated the future employment of a "sudden-concentrate-sudden-disperse" strategy that would allow the PLA to make the most of its newfound superiority by eliminating selected nationalist army groups in a conventional battle. To his credit, Su had already shown that a conventional battle could be won, making the PLA supreme decision-making organ, the Central Military Commission, more than willing to adopt Su's plan. With the fall of Jinan on 24 September, Su seized the moment. The capture of Jinan and the evacuation of Kaifeng allowed for assaults to be conducted along virtually the whole stretch of the Jinpu railway line. The desired outcome of these activities was achieved when considerably large KMT forces were lured to Xuzhou where the PLA was wreaking havoc.

The Jinpu line was of great strategic value, as it was the main route to the Yangtze River and Nanking, the birthplace of the KMT and site of the tomb of the revered father of modern China, Dr Sun Yat-sen. On 3 November, Huang Baitao stressed to his commander Liu Zhi the urgent need to bring in more troops to defend the railway line. Intelligence reports that indicated the powerful East China and Central Plains field armies were marching on the line, strengthened Huang's case. Albeit that Liu was an experienced commander, he procrastinated, deciding to first consult with Nanking liaison officer, Du Yuming. Two days later, orders were received to reinforce the Jinpu line.

Alarm and confusion permeated the KMT's military offices in Nanking. Military defeat at the hands of the communists appeared imminent. Despondent residents of the city could no longer believe in KMT talk of "victories and strategic withdrawals". The painful reality was that Chiang's armies were sustaining disastrous reverses south of Hsuchow, reverses that Chiang could no longer prevent. Nationalist forces southwest of Hsuchow had been completely enveloped by the PLA; it was now only a matter of when they would be crushed. Radio reports claimed that, among others, the Twelfth Army Group had already met such a fate.

Nanking knew that the dregs of the nationalist forces falling back south of the Yangtze would not be able to defend the city against Mao's red tidal wave.

In northern China, the fluid situation was as dire as the PLA struck toward Peiping. At the time, the communists were already active along the Peiping–Kalgan railway line. Communication between the two points had become tenuous as powerful PLA units threatened both flanks of the line. For the KMT, the exact objectives of the PLA, or of their own forces for that matter, had become totally clouded, and uncertainty prevailed. Word had been received that the evacuation of Kalgan had been ordered, but no one appeared to know under whose authority.

Senior staff at the Kalgan (Zhangjiakou) coal mines had reported that Tangshan and the mine area, 190 miles to the southeast, had been evacuated and subsequently occupied by the PLA. That left nearby Tianjin as the only mining operation able to supply coal, but nowhere sufficient to meet demand.

The Pingjin Campaign resulted in the communist conquest of northern China. Lasting sixty-four days, from 21 November 1948 to 31 January 1949, the PLA sustained heavy casualties while taking Zhangjiakou and Tianjin, together with its port and garrison at Dagu and Peiping. The communists had redeployed 890,000 troops from the northeast to face around 600,000 KMT troops. The PLA suffered 40,000 casualties at Zhangjiakou alone, but in turn they accounted for an estimated 520,000 KMT killed, wounded or captured during the campaign.

By the winter of 1948, the balance of power in northern China was swinging in favour of the People's Liberation Army. As the PLA Fourth Field Army, commanded by Lin Biao and Luo Ronghuan, entered the North China Plain at the close of the Liaoshen Campaign, Fu Zuoyi and the KMT government in Nanking abandoned Chengde, Baoding, Shanhai Pass and Qinhuangdao, while simultaneously withdrawing the remaining nationalist troops to Peiping, Tianjin and Zhangjiakou to strengthen the defences of these garrisons. The KMT was hoping to preserve its strength by reinforcing Xuzhou where another communist campaign was being waged, or alternatively retreat to nearby Suiyuan Province if forced to do so.

While gearing up for the campaign, the PLA stemmed the advance of the First Field Army towards Taiyuan. The attack on Hohhot was also stalled as the Third Field Army was being deployed from Jining District toward Peiping.

On 29 November, the PLA launched an attack on Zhangjiakou. Fu Zuoyi immediately ordered the KMT 35th Army in Peiping and the 104th Army in Huailai to reinforce the city. On 2 December, the PLA Second Field Army started to approach Zhuolu, while the PLA Fourth Field Army took Miyun on 5 December, before striking out toward Huailai. At the same time, the Second Field Army advanced on Zhuolu from the south. As Peiping was in the risk of being encircled, Fu recalled both the 35th and 104th armies from Zhangjiakou to return and support the defence of Peiping before being "surrounded and destroyed" by the PLA.

On its return, the nationalist 35th Army found itself surrounded by PLA forces at Xinbao'an. Nationalist reinforcements dispatched from Peiping were intercepted by the communists before they reach the beleaguered city. In the rapidly deteriorating situation, the desperate Fu Zuoyi attempted covert

Mao and his third wife, He Jijen.

negotiations with the CCP on 14 December, but his approaches were spurned five days later. On 21 December, the PLA launched a final massed attack on the city, resulting in its capitulation the following evening. Guo Jingyun, defeated commander of the 35th Army, took his own life as the PLA forces flooded into the city. Whatever remained of the garrison was annihilated as it desperately tried to escape back to Zhangjiakou.

After taking both Zhangjiakou and Xinbao'an, on 2 January 1949, the PLA began to concentrate troops in the Tianjin surrounds. With the victorious conclusion of the Huaihai Campaign to the south, on 14 January the PLA launched a final attack on Tianjin. After twenty-nine hours of bitter fighting, the KMT 62nd and 86th armies and a total of 130,000 men in ten divisions were either killed or captured, including the KMT commander Chen Changjie. Remnants of KMT troops from the 17th Army Group and the 87th Army fled south and escaped by sea on 17 January.

The fall of Tianjin effectively left the KMT garrison in Peiping completely cut off from other nationalist forces. Fu Zuoyi, knowing he had run out of options, commenced peace negotiations with the PLA on 21 January. A few days later, around 260,000 nationalist troops began leaving the city in anticipation of an immediate surrender. On 31 January, the PLA Fourth Field Army marched into Peiping to claim another people's victory, and in doing so, marked the end of the campaign.

After the successful Liaoshen, Huaihai and Pingjin campaigns, the PLA accounted for 144 regular and 29 irregular KMT divisions, including 1.54 million battle-experienced KMT troops. This effectively marked the end of the KMT army. Stalin, however, was desirous of a coalition government in China, so he tried to prevent Mao from crossing the Yangtze River and moving south. Mao ignored Stalin's stance, and on 21 April his troops crossed the river. Two days later, Mao claimed his biggest prize of the war to date: Nanking, the KMT's citadel. Chiang's government then embarked a on a series of retreats: first to Canton until 15 October, then Chongqing until 25 November, and then Chengdu before finally leaving the mainland for the island of Taiwan on 10 December.

By late 1949, the PLA was mopping up remnants of KMT forces in southern China, leaving only Tibet. The Kuomintang made several final desperate attempts to use Khampa Tibetan troops against the communists in southwestern China. A plan was drawn up in which three Khampa divisions would be

Chinese Red Army now only 40 Miles from Hong Kong

Nationalists Preparing for 'Dunkirk'

Hong Kong, Saturday: Chinese Communists are to-day in control of the city of Canton, only 80 miles from Hong Kong. All communications between Canton and the Crown Colony have been cut and fighting is said to be in progress 40 miles from British soil. It is expected Communist troops will reach the Hong Kong border some time to-night.

Chinese press reports say that Nationalist troops have abandoned their positions on the mainland border of Hong Kong. They are stated to be withdrawing westward for evacuation by sea.

Later to-day Communist guerrillas occupied Sha Tau Kok, on the eastern end of the frontier between Hong Kong and China. British patrols along the border were reinforced.

In Hong Kong, British Government and military officials called conferences to discuss the situation in Canton. They were particularly concerned with Communists elements inside the Crown Colony. The strength of these elements is indicated by the number of Communist flags displayed.

City Tense

There are 112 Britons, mainly missionaries, still in Canton. The city is said to be quiet by tense.

One Communist column, north of Canton, was to-day reported to be driving towards the north bank of the Singkiang River, in an attempt to cut off the Nationalist retreat corridor westward.

The river ship Fatshan, last ship to leave Canton yesterday, arrived in Hong Kong with a full load of evacuees. Among the passengers were a handful of British businessmen and missionaries and a Salvation Army officer.

Yorkshire Evening Post, Saturday, 15 October 1949

supported by the Buddhist 10th Panchen Lama, Gonpo Tseten, to oppose the communists from a base in southwestern China. The independently minded Panchen Lama, however, elected to withdraw his endorsement, defecting to the communists instead.

Shanghai, the commercial capital of China, fell to the Communists in late May. After the capture of Wuhan in May, the PLA forces were split for the final assault on remaining KMT territory. One force, led by Peng Dehuai, marched westward from Wuhan towards Xi'an and Lanzhou; both fell in August 1949. Another PLA force led by Lin Biao struck south toward Canton (Guangzhou), which was taken in October, while part of Lin Biao's force was sent southwestward to clean up remaining pockets of KMT resistance in Guizhou and Chongqing, both of which were captured in November.

Earlier in 1949, in an unpublished document produced by a well-known CCP organization in Hong Kong, the Yau Lee Printing Company, Li Chi-shen appealed to Whampoa Military Academy students and graduates, and officers and men of the KMT to desert the Chiang government and follow the leadership of the Kuomintang Revolutionary Committee (KUTRC). The document was never printed in local Hong Kong newspapers, so it appears likely that the Chinese Communists distributed it for propaganda purposes.

Extolling their right to be called 'revolutionary soldiers' after overthrowing the northern warlords in 1926 and their unfaltering resistance to Japanese occupation, Li accused Chiang of having violated Sun Yat-sen's political philosophy embodied in 'Three People's Principles'—*Minzu, Minquan,* and *Minsheng,* defined as nationalism, democracy, and the livelihood of the people)—and adopting fascism:

> He not only persecuted the people and oppressed the KMT members who had struggled desperately for the country, but also usurped the party and the nation. For his own selfish end, he prolonged the civil war and drained the country of its resources, which led to the Japanese Imperialists' aggression in the Northeast. After the Manchurian Incident, persisting in his dictatorial rule, he ordered the Northeast Army not to resist, and concluded many disgraceful pacts with the Japanese Imperialists, incurring the loss of sovereignty. He suppressed all anti-Japanese movements, both in word and deed, and disbanded the anti-Japanese forces.
>
> What did you do? Did you comply with the aims of the late Dr Sun to save the nation and her people, or were you the tools of Chiang Kai-shek to harm the nation and her people?

Li accused the "atrocious, corrupt, and exploiting Chiang government" of having "deprived the peasants, workers, industrialists, merchants, culturists, educationists, liberal professionists [sic] and civil servants of their living" by surrendering their sovereign rights to American imperialists. They had collaborated with the remnants of Japanese imperialism to suppress the resistance put up by "compatriots". He added that the "dictatorial and traitorous" government of Chiang was hated not only by the communists, but by all the people of China.

> Chiang's policy is contradictory to the late Dr Sun's aims and to the original principles and policy of the KMT. Chiang Kai-shek's so-called 'Rebellion Suppression' is a struggle to prolong his dictatorial and traitorous rule and maintain the fascist group. It is not a war for the protection of the KMT; Chiang's government cannot represent the KMT. In the present civil war, which is not a dispute between the Nationalists and the Communists, there are two camps—a group of landlords, bureaucrats and compradores headed by Chiang Kai-shek, who uses armed force to suppress the people, and a democratic united front, representing the people who oppose suppression by armed force.

On 1 October 1949, Mao Zedong proclaimed the birth of the People's Republic of China with its capital at Peiping, which returned to its former name, Beijing.

Saluting the people's hero with their little red books.

6. THE BIG THREE

To the victor the spoils, and with the final demise of the KMT, in June 1949 the CCP announced the ideological methodology for the ultimate neutralization of all KMT structures and what they stood for. In its stead, would be the communist roadmap:

1. We must thoroughly understand the role of taking over.

   Taking over is the beginning of control. It means enlarging the properties of bureaucratic capitalists and turning them into properties of the people. It is turning what was used for the benefit of feudalists, compradors and bureaucratic capitalists in the past, to the service of the people of today. This is entirely different from the procedure of the KMT after the Japanese surrender, when they, by their corrupt practices, stole the fruits of the people's victory and divided the properties taken over.

2. In carrying out the work of taking over, the following principle should be observed.

   In taking over the investments of bureaucratic capitalists, we should preserve the original enterprising machineries in their entirety, with their original techniques and productive system. We should smash the political machineries, and reform the cultural machineries of the K.P. taken over. Our policy in taking over should be:

   "To maintain the original investment machineries, abolish the bureaucratic monopoly system, strengthen supervision, and safeguard production."

3. Preparation in thought.

   We should understand that taking over is the beginning of government. It is political warfare, and a new and complex task. Therefore, on the one hand we should maintain an adequate war spirit and be alert in politics; on the other hand, we should have patience in inquiries and studies.

4. Policy.
   a. A policy of confiscating bureaucratic capital and protecting individual capital should be adopted.

b. A correct attitude toward the old staff should be assumed. We should first utilize them in the handing over. Those who have merit will be rewarded, while corrupt officials will be punished. After the taking over, those who wish to quit will be accorded a farewell, while those who wish to remain will be welcome.

c. A policy of propaganda education in combined politics and techniques, for the education of the old staff, should be adopted so as to promote and safeguard the work of the people.

5. Preparation for organization.
   a. Unity and concentration of leadership.
   b. Cadre should first conduct concentration, distribution and education.
   c. Preparation should be made for all sorts of cadres who are familiar with the work. They should be organized separately. We should have cadres to conduct the taking over and cadres to carry out routine work. Prior to and in the course of taking over, we should keep in touch with, write and absorb the old staff.

6. Preparation for work.
   a. Objectives of taking over should be fixed separately.
   b. Inquiry into conditions of studies.
   c. Different preparatory resolutions with regard to taking over should be drafted. This is to estimate the different states or affairs which might possibly occur after entering cities. They are to be used according to changes in the situation.
   d. The important point of taking over is staff; but the order of taking over is properties first, then documents, and lastly staff.
   e. Stages in the course of taking over.
      1st stage: Concentration of officials for taking over, making preparations for all work for taking over.
      2nd stage: To seal by sections, adjust and examine.
      3rd stage: To sum up.

7. Disciplinary education should be strengthened.
   a. Conception of service for the people should be strengthened.
   b. To seek for instruction beforehand and make report after the work is completed.
   c. To lead a decent life.

Central Intelligence Agency, 30 June 1949

Chairman Mao.

"'BIG THREE' WILL RULE 'NEW' CHINA," the British newspaper *Daily Herald* proclaimed in its Monday, 3 October 1949 edition. "The newest of the world's Communists regimes, established in Peiping last Friday, will be controlled by the same 'big three' who have led China from the wilderness to dazzling military triumphs."

Correspondent Hessell Tiltman, in a world that was starting to freefall into an international crisis labelled the 'Cold War', gave a refreshingly honest—many would argue naïve—biographical cameo of the three communists who steered an ambitious people's revolution to a victorious People's Republic of China (PRC):

No. 1 is plump, 56-year-old Mao Tse-tung, a peasant son of peasants who has been China's "Yellow Lenin" for the past 22 years.

The tough Mao once declared "a revolution isn't an invitation to a banquet," and his own road to power has not been any banquet either. One of his wives was caught and executed by Chinese Nationalists. Mao led the Communists in the famous year-long 6,000 mile "long march" from South China to the inaccessible North-West in the 1930s to escape encirclement by the Nationalist forces.

He himself walked almost the whole distance with the survivors who established themselves in the cave city of Yanan. There Mao lived with his fourth wife, who is a photogenic Chinese film star, in a mud hut in summer and in caves in winter. He has never been out of China, and still wears the simple garb of a peasant and talks like one.

China's Mao Received by Stalin

Praises Aid to Liberation

The Chinese Communist leader, Mao Tse-tung, has arrived in Moscow, Moscow radio reported last night.

Mao was received by Marshal Stalin at a meeting at which Mr. Vishinsky, the Soviet Foreign Minister was present. Mao was met by Mr. Molotov, Marshal Bulganin, and the Deputy Foreign Minister, Mr. Gromyko.

In a speech at the railway station. Mao spoke warmly of Russian "aid to the cause of Chinese liberation." A guard of honour welcomed him at the station, which was decorated with flags of their new Chinese Communist Government. Mao was also met by Czech, Korean, Bulgarian, Rumanian, Hungarian, Mongolian, Albanian, Polish, and East German diplomats.

U.S. Generals' Mission

Meanwhile, two United States generals arrived at Saigon, in Indo-China, yesterday, to discuss with the French High Commissioners and Service chiefs the consequences of France's recognition of the Chinese Communist Government.

They were Lieut.-Gen. George Stratemeyer, the American Air Force C-in-C, Far East, and Maj.-Gen. Charles Willoughby, Personal Assistant to Gen. MacArthur, the Supreme Allied Commander in the Pacific.

They had previously visited Singapore for talks with Mr. Malcolm MacDonald, the British High Commissioner for South-East Asia, and had had Pacific defence talks there and in Hong Kong with British Commanders.

Western Morning News, Saturday, 17 December 1949

For weeks past persistent rumours have been circulating in Pekin [sic] that Mao was a sick man, afflicted with either diabetes or with a heart ailment. But informants who have seen him at close range within the past few months declare that he looked bronzed and fit, and recent Communist-taken close-up photographs of Mao depict the tough Communist chieftain as tough as ever.

Zhou Enlai, 1924.

The second of the big three mentioned by Tiltman is Zhou Enlai, an articulate diplomat who served as the new nation's foreign minister from 1949 to 1958. Zhou was largely responsible for orchestrating US President Richard Nixon's visit to China in February 1972, the first by an American president.

No. 2 is Chou En-lai, first premier of Red China.

Chou is a suave, urbane, strikingly handsome and mentally agile intellectual, educated in Japan and France.

During General Marshall's 1946 peace talks in Nanking, Chou, who headed the Communist delegation, became famous among newspaper men for his marathon Press conferences which sometimes lasted five hours or more, with Chou doing all the talking throughout. Chou is well versed in Western history and ideas and gets on well with people.

Since the Communists took Peking, he has been the only high-up in the Red hierarchy accessible even to the most favoured foreign visitors to the city.

His appointment to the Premiership is seen by some as ensuring representation within the highest Communist Government councils for the view of the so-called "moderate" wing of the Chinese Communist Party. This wing is reported to favour limited cooperation with foreign businessmen in China, at least for the present, provided that it is on terms laid down by the Communists.

Chou is also widely tipped as the probable leader of the first Chinese Communist delegation to the United Nations if the Communist regime wins international recognition.

The third key figure in the regime was General Zhu De (Chu-Teh), a graduate from a military academy who, in his early life, had enlisted in a rebel army, soon becoming a warlord. He served as commander-in-chief of the Eighth Route Army during the Second Sino-Japanese War.

No. 3 is General Chu-Teh, 63-year-old strategist who is the chief architect of the "liberation army's" military successes and has the reputation earned the hard way, of being one of China's greatest military leaders and a foremost authority on guerrilla warfare. Born the son of wealthy parents [his family were in fact poor; he was adopted by a wealthy uncle when he was nine], Chu-Teh started life as an official in Yunnan Province, where he lived in a palatial mansion, smoked opium and kept a flock of concubines.

In his early twenties he suddenly gave up his mansion, opium and concubines and went on a pilgrimage to Europe.

In Paris he embraced Communism and then moved on to Moscow, where he studied for some time.

Back in China he joined up with Mao Tse-tung, and in 1931, shortly before the Long March, he became C-in-C of the Chinese Red Army, a position he continues to hold in the new Government, of which he is one of the six vice-Chairmen.

On 10 October 1949, the victorious CCP leaders were crowded on the balcony of the Gate of Heavenly Peace, or Tiananmen, known for its symbolism in future passive resistance to communist rule. Spread out before them was a panoramic view of Peiping, which had survived the war more or less unscathed. This was to be the new capital with a new regime, which was now congregating, hence the pomp and the desire for a formal occasion. At the Gate of Heavenly Peace, microphones and cameras were prepared as the city's residents assembled, jubilant after having endured months of siege. It was impossible to see Mao himself over the teeming throng, but an enormous poster portrait of the new leader was unfurled from the balcony where he stood, a harbinger of the hero-worship propaganda cult that was to become integral to communism in China and elsewhere. Everyone, it seemed, was aware that a new era so different from the decades under the KMT was about to begin. To celebrate the auspicious occasion, the PLA laid on a Soviet-style parade of columns of marching troops and fighting vehicles that would have done Moscow's Red Square proud.

Attired in his signature buttoned-up jacket and flanked by his staff, Mao read out the proclamation creating the People's Republic of China, and itemizing the newly appointed ministers and their portfolios.

To reach this final triumphant point of the revolution, Mao had endured numerous personal sacrifices in his quest: the execution of his second wife Yang Kaihui in 1930, the loss of three of his children during the Long March, while his son Anying, grew up on his own in the Soviet Union, a guest of the Stalin regime. Ironically—or coincidentally—Chiang Kai-shek's only son, Ching-kuo, had a similar experience in the Soviet Union, and even married a Russian woman.

For a long time after the success of the people's revolution, Western political analysts and intelligence organs debated the extent, if any, to which Moscow determined the course of the fledgling communist state.

Mao's foreign policy, according to a declassified report of 8 March 1950, was tempered by the theory that capitalist nations would act coldly at best and with hostility at worst toward a communist-controlled country. Both he and Zhou Enlai, at least on 'emotional grounds', believed that this theory was false with respect to China, so they were willing to develop relations with the Western powers. By doing so, however, they would imperil their friendship with the Soviet Union.

However, a belief that China's foreign policy should be based on a united front among communist states against the capitalist West was held by the pro-Moscow faction in the CCP, which was led by Liu Shaoqi. The group held that China had to subjugate her national requirements to those of the Soviet Union, because it was imperative to assist Moscow in its position as the bastion of international revolution. Seldom expressed in print, this view was however, inherently implicit in all Sino-Soviet propaganda dealing with Sino-Soviet relations. For most, this was proof that Chinese national propaganda was largely controlled by the Soviet faction in the party.

The strength of this pro-Soviet faction was sufficient to prevent Mao from acting independently of it, particularly when it came to foreign relations. To neutralize this influence, Mao appointed people loyal to him personally to key positions—adherents referred to in the party as the Yanan Communists.

However, for Mao, the immediate post-liberation period was a constant struggle with Liu and his disciples, who incessantly hampered Mao's working relationships with Western nations, while applying all their resources to secure and strengthen Moscow's influence in China.

Liu Shaoqi's popularity, however, did not wane, his powerful influence remaining a thorn in Mao and the Yanan Communists' flesh. In 1959,

Liu succeeded Mao as president of the People's Republic of China, and into the 1960s, he continued to usurp Mao's status. In spite of the fact that Liu chaired a special politburo meeting to launch the Cultural Revolution in 1966, a programme to purge the party of corruption and red tape and restore to it the true communist ideals of Sun Yat-sen and the liberation war, the resultant purge would see his total demise.

Mao seized the opportunity to subvert the reformation into a pro-Maoist revolution, with the objectives of creating a monopoly of power and eradicating even his perceived enemies. Labelled a "traitor' and a "capitalist roader", an "enemy agent and scab in the service of the imperialists", Liu, a long-term sufferer of

China Makes It

China has exploded her first thermos-nuclear device—or, put in popular language, China now has the hydrogen bomb. It is not a dramatic happening, so Britain and a considerable part of the world will have little difficulty in taking no notice of it. That highly developed human defence mechanism which enable us to disregard external events, giving the comfortable reassurance that all is well and there is no message for us in them, will come smoothly into operation.

Circumstances favour passive lack of interest. Some weeks ago the United States announced that China would shortly be detonating another device and that it might well be a thermos-nuclear device. The known loses its terrors: by using the term "conventional nuclear weapon," we persuade ourselves that we have to come to terms with the old-fashioned atomic bomb that destroyed Hiroshima and Nagasaki.

China, which exploded its first atomic weapon in 1964, and its second last year, has not been particularly fast in developing nuclear potential, though it has just preceded France in providing itself with a thermos-nuclear weapon. France is expected to follow suit this summer. But a delay of a year or two makes no difference, nor does the fact that China at present possesses no means of "delivering" an atomic or hydrogen bomb on enemy territory. As the years go by, it can be expected to develop rockets.

> The fact that has to be faced by the Soviet Union no less that the United States and the rest of the world is that within a decade or so China, the country with the world's largest population, will effectively possess the ultimate weapon. At the moment this knowledge affects Communist China's policy negatively, in the sense that it is unlikely that she would take overt military action against the United States in Vietnam. If she did, America could retaliate by bombing China's nuclear development plants and so retard, if not prohibit, attainment of nuclear parity.
>
> But what sort of neighbour will China be to the world when she does reach parity within a decade or 15 years? It cannot be doubted that China will be much more assertive. What is immensely dangerous for world peace is that China's millions are being brought up with an intense hatred of America. The overwhelming Chinese hatred of the United States is going to be a tremendously powerful factor in human destiny. One of the most turbulent periods in all human history would appear to be before us. Whatever can be done to lessen the explosive possibilities must be done at this stage, which is why Britain must arouse itself from its stupor of indifference.
>
> *Birmingham Daily Post*, Tuesday, 10 May 1966

diabetes, died on 12 November 1969, after having endured successive bouts of pneumonia as a result of his declining immune system. Many accused the Mao regime of orchestrating Liu's death through medical maltreatment. Liu was cremated the day after his death.

Mao Zedong died on 9 September 1976 at the age of 82, leaving no clear successor to take over leadership of 800 million Chinese. It is most unlikely that such a venerated individual with such supreme power would again lead the Chinese peoples. For many, however, the demigod myth evaporated with Mao's brutal interpretation of the premises of the Cultural Revolution.

Together with the death of Zhou Enlai in January 1976 and that of General Chu Teh in July that year, the departure of Mao created a power vacuum that had been further compounded by the purging in April of Deng Xiaoping.

Zhu De, Yanan, 1940.

During the Cultural Revolution of 1966 to 1976, the notorious Gang of Four emerged in the Communist Party of China to control the party's organs of power. Led by Mao's last wife, Jian Qing, the group—the others being Zhang Chunqiao, Yao Wenyuan, and Wang Hangmen—behaved and made decisions that, at times, were indistinguishable from those of Mao. It therefore came as little surprise, only a month after Mao's death, that his successor, pro-Maoist Hua Guofeng, had the Gang of Four removed from office and arrested.

Late in 1978, Long March veteran and reformist, Deng Xiaoping, ousted Hua and dismantled the last vestiges of Mao's Cultural Revolution. By 1982, Deng's policy of allowing public criticism of the ruling machinery and his desire for deep reforms had culminated in a declaration by the party's central committee stating that Mao's class-struggle doctrines and mass public campaigns could no longer play a part in China's chosen route for the future. Economic reform topped Deng's agenda for China, bringing down the bamboo curtain to international trade and a liberalization of the nation's economy, embodied in the vision of 'Four Modernizations'—agriculture, industry, science and technology, and the military.

On 1 January 1979, the United States recognized the People's Republic of China, closely followed by an official visit by Deng to Washington, the citadel of the once-loathed capitalist enemy of the people's China.

Deng Xiaoping and President Jimmy Carter after signing the Sino-American Treaty, 31 January 1979. (Photo US NARA)

7. EASTERN SUPERPOWER

That China is one of the world's four Great Powers is an absolute farce. I have told the [US] President I would be reasonably polite about this American obsession, but I cannot agree that we should take a positive attitude on this matter.

The latest information from inside China points to the rise already of a rival Government to supplant Chiang Kai-shek, and now there is always a Communist civil war impending there. While not opposing the President's wish, I should object very much if we adopted other than a perfectly negative line, leaving him to do the needful with the Russians.

Winston Churchill, 23 August 1944, to his foreign secretary about a suggested meeting of foreign ministers on future world organization.

Chinese People's Volunteer Army POWs captured by US Marines in Korea, December 1950. (Photo USMC)

A year after the People's Republic of China declared its existence, its forces were ploughing through North Korea to drive the United Nations forces away from the Yalu River. General Peng Dehuai was entrusted with saving Kim Il-sung's regime as a matter of grand strategy—holding Korea would secure Manchuria. Kim with thousands of Koreans had fought hand in hand with the People's Volunteer Army (PVA) in 1949—now it was China's opportunity to reciprocate.

The PVA's participation in the Korean War was the first and only conflict when Chinese and American-led UN forces have clashed in conventional warfare. Initially, the PVA, drawn from the PLA, enjoyed the advantage provided by its seasoned commanders whose combat experience and discipline were very evident. With the stalemate at the 38th Parallel, the PVA's shortcomings became visible, especially when confronted with American determination and superior air support. The indecisive Korean conflict, halted with an indeterminate ceasefire in Panmunjom, cost the PVA a million soldiers.

In 1950, the PLA moved to annex Tibet, and in the following year, in return for proscribed autonomy, the 14th Dalai Lama was forced "under duress" to sign the Seventeen Point Agreement for the Peaceful Liberation of Tibet, affirming communist Chinese sovereignty over Tibet. In a short space of time, Beijing had entered into a confident period of territorial expansion.

The irony was rich, for a communist state founded on anti-colonialism and democracy was now imposing itself on foreign soil. What was becoming obvious to anyone familiar with Chinese history was Beijing's newfound confidence in territorial expansion along the lines of the Qing Dynasty.

It should also be borne in mind that the bitter feud with the Kuomintang, now ensconced in Taiwan, had not officially been brought to a finite conclusion. PLA commanders continued to look east, believing that the Kinmen and Matsu island groups had to be taken in preparation for an all-out assault on Taiwan, officially the Republic of China dominated by the KMT, which had been forced off the mainland at the end of the civil war. However, during the Battle of Guningtou in October 1949, the KMT repelled an invasion of Kinmen by Chinese communist forces.

In Taiwan itself, the KMT's brutal quashing of a civilian uprising on 28 February 1947 and institution of martial law, signalled more than thirty-eight years of what became known as the 'White Terror'. During the longest period of martial law in the world at the time, 140,000 Taiwanese were incarcerated and as many as 4,000 executed for any apparent communist leanings. Under the clumsily titled

120,000 Chinese Face Allies in Korea

Enemy Has Plenty of Ammunition
Communists, who had weathered the first assault of the Allied limited offensive in Korea, suddenly relaxed today and, in one place west of Chorwon gave up a hill disputed for a week.

Everywhere along the battleline British and U.S. forces, who launched the offensive on Wednesday, reported only light to moderate resistance where, for two days, Communist resistance has been unvaryingly heavy.

There was no reason given for the enemy's sudden relaxation. At some places along the United Nations' line of advance there was little or no contact with Communists. Chinese troops—there are 120,000 of them—who opposed the Allied assault seemed fresh and well-equipped. For the first time in sustained battle they were not short of ammunition.

Blanketed by thousands of shells from the massed batteries of British, New Zealand and Canadian 25-pound guns, the hill and ridges appeared lifeless as the [King's Own Scottish] Borderers began their advance. But the Chinese, dug deeply in the earth, waited. Two hours later they hit back with machine guns, carbines, grenades, and their own artillery and mortars.

Then the "battle of the woods" began. It continued without pause throughout the burning hot day, through the bitterly cold night and most of the next day.—Reuter and British United Press.

Yorkshire Evening Post, Friday, 5 October 1951

constitutional provision 'Temporary Provisions Effective During the Period of National Mobilization for Suppression of the Communist Rebellion', effective from 1948, Chiang Kai-shek effectively nullified the constitution and established martial law in Taiwan, where civil and political freedoms were severely restricted. The official rationale for this forced imposition of a one-party state was given as the ongoing Chinese Civil War, Chiang firmly convinced that it would take KMT forces only three years to reclaim mainland China from the communists. In 1965, Project National Glory was launched to prepare the Taiwanese armed forces for an invasion of the mainland. However, after a few tentative sorties into communist Chinese territorial waters were surgically dealt with by the People's Liberation Army Navy, Taiwan's designs on the mainland fizzled out in mid-1972.

In 1971, the United Nations voted in favour of replacing the representative of Taiwan with that of the People's Republic of China as the legal representative of China.

On 5 April 1975, Generalissimo Chiang Kai-shek, after having suffered a heart attack earlier in the year, died in Taipei twenty-six years after the Kuomintang fled to Taiwan. He was 87 years old. By the early 1990s, the Kuomintang finally lost its status as head of a military dictatorship when multi-party democracy arrived in Taiwan.

As the second largest economy by nominal GDP behind the US, with a ballooning annual defence budget for its rapidly modernizing armed forces, China ranks far lower in other conventional metrics. It is also bogged down by problems at home and abroad.

Worryingly, in the region China staunchly acts as protecting communist brother to international pariah and nuclear-armed North Korea, whose existence

Escorted by Deng Xiaoping, US President Gerald Ford arrives at Peking Capital Airport, December 1975.

it has bankrolled—and tolerated—for several decades. The same enduring time span is shared with its simmering rivalry with its wayward 'province', Taiwan.

Never before in human history have a succession of brutal and undemocratic regimes managed to control 1.4 billion people with such apparent ease. It may be argued that China has just been made attractive by the wonder of its newfound wealth. Underneath the steel and concrete and propaganda is a totalitarian state obsessed with control.

Can this unprecedented track record in world civilization be traced back to Mao Zedong and the dismantling of the nationalist Kuomintang? Nothing in the historical record suggests that the Great Helmsman's leadership set the People's Republic of China on its current path.

Until his death in 1976, the political excesses of the Cultural Revolution and the Gang of Four perpetuated the doctrines of Mao's style of Marxist-Leninism. Governance was largely dictatorial in an artificial vacuum created by self-imposed international economic and cultural isolationism. The impotent Hua Guofeng provided rudderless leadership, a period characterized by rapid intra-party corruption, subterfuge and jealousies.

Arguably, the global superpower that is modern China was spawned by the outward-looking visions of the progressive Deng Xiaoping. Twice the victim of CCP purges, Deng overnight catapulted China onto the world stage. Assuming power in 1978, Deng opened vast swathes of unutilized land in China's southern provinces and coastal cities, and invited foreign companies, mostly from North America, to relocate their low-cost jobs in these vast industrial parks.

In a short space of time, China developed a burgeoning economy, in sharp contrast to the stagnation of the Mao era, dominated by archaic state-owned heavy industry. Mao was driven by a dogmatic need to free China from foreign and internal aggressors, particularly the Japanese and the KMT. This was best achieved through the use of force, brainwashing and coercion—millions would perish in the names of the Great Leap Forward and the Cultural Revolution.

Deng Xiaoping stepped down in 1993, passing the baton onto a successor Jiang Zemin, whose watch saw the peaceful transfer of Hong Kong back to China in 1997. To dampen tensions between the former territory's citizens and the mainland's authoritarian system, the city was made a Special Administrative Region under the 'One Country, Two Systems' doctrine that preserved Hong Kong's status as a financial centre and an investor's gateway into the Chinese market.

After Jiang came the even more reserved President Hu Jintao, whose time in office saw China's miracle overheat and almost sputter when a housing crisis in the United States rocked the global financial system. China's reaction to the crisis between 2007 and 2009 is a startling example of its resilience during momentous crisis. Rather than allow foreign investment to disappear and run dry, Beijing launched an epic stimulus programme that allowed the provincial governments, some of which had local economies equal to small countries, access to low-interest loans for infrastructure building.

In 2012, leadership was passed to Xi Jinping who inaugurated his presidency with a broad anti-corruption crackdown. Among the pitfalls of a one-party state—so much more a one-party dictatorship—is the rampant corruption in the bureaucracy. China's intricate system of governance is no exception, and state-controlled news played a vital role publicizing each high-profile CCP member who was arrested.

There are two salient features that make Xi's tenure different from those of his antecedents. First, China's economy is growing at a slower pace compared

A full US military arrival ceremony welcomes Xi Jinping to the Pentagon, 14 February 2012.

to the 1990s and 2000s. Second, there is a more pronounced nationalist hysteria in the public sphere, a sentiment that boiled over when Beijing began claiming the remote Diaoyu Islands owned by Japan when Xi entered office. The controversy sparked some of the worst outbreaks of xenophobic anti-Japanese rioting in decades.

Since becoming China's undisputed leader, Xi appears to have deftly navigated through both these problems and made them into cornerstones of his rule. Chinese nationalism, rather than Maoism, is the new state ideology and as such is being shaped and directed by the government to give citizens a sentiment they should fixate on rather than dwell on real issues like corruption, the absence of democracy, and myriad social ills.

The Soviet Union's dissolution was actually a boon for China because it neutralized a rival with an immense nuclear arsenal and a mechanized army that threatened Beijing. It is no wonder the US, along with other NATO members, agreed to share military technology with China from 1984 till 1989. Ronald Reagan's administration drew up plans for tanks, fighter jets, transport planes, helicopters, and missiles to be co-produced with China's own military-industrial complex. But the fallout from Tiananmen Square brought an abrupt halt to these initiatives.

In the 1990s, Beijing and Moscow normalized relationships and became all-weather trade partners, so much so that scores of fourth-generation Sukhoi Su-27 'Flanker' fighter aircraft (with a licence to produce the Shenyang J-11 version) and 'Kilo' class diesel-electric attack submarines were sold to China in multi-billion-dollar deals that effectively negated the US-led arms embargo.

It is therefore not surprising that Chinese companies were later able to reverse-engineer these high-tech Russian weapons platforms and systems to produce local versions. The Sino-Russian alliance hasn't receded either. The militaries of either country hold joint drills on a regular basis, while Beijing remains a serious customer for Russian technology, including the advanced S-400 Triumf (SA-21 'Growler') air defence system and joint ventures in aerospace production.

In 1998, construction work began on permanent structures erected over reefs and other natural features in the South China Sea, setting a precedent that would inflame maritime disputes with China's neighbours well into the following century. Chinese barges commenced dredging operations in the South China Sea in 2012, in what transpired to be construction work for

Crushing the 'Counter Revolution'

The power struggle among China's leaders, set off by weeks of pro-democracy protests in Peking, was won by the conservative old guard—those like Prime Minister Li Peng, loyal to 84-year-old Deng Xiaoping. At about 2am on June 3 some 10,000 soldiers of the People's Liberation Army, apparently unarmed, attempted to clear Peking's Tiananmen Square, the focal point of pro-democracy protests. But they were routed by protestors, just as they had been on their previous attempt on May 19. Humiliated, they retreated among cries of "Long live the people!" and "The People's Army loves the people!"

But on the following day the People's Army turned on the people. In the early hours of June 4 about 100,000 soldiers, armed this time with automatic rifles and backed up by more than 200 tanks and by armoured personnel carriers, stormed Tiananmen Square. Firing indiscriminately on unarmed protestors, the troops killed at least 1,000 people, although the exact number of casualties will never be known: it was widely believed that unrecovered bodies littering the square and the Avenue of Eternal Peace were gathered into pyres by the soldiers and burnt. Many of those killed were crushed under the wheels of armoured vehicles.

Although the army effectively regained control of the square in a matter of hours, sporadic shooting and killing continued in central Peking throughout June 4 and for several more days.

On June 8, Li Peng—one of the leaders most consistently criticised by the protestors—made his first public appearance since the weekend carnage. Shown on television congratulating troops, he told them: "I hope you continue to work hard to preserve peace and order in the capital."

Illustrated London News, Saturday, 1 July 1989

permanent air-naval facilities on 'artificial islands' equipped with radars and anti-aircraft batteries.

Over the same period, diplomatic relations with nationalist Taiwan improved, but there was no commensurate reduction of PLA forces based in Fujian, 130 miles

PLA navy vessels in Dong Hai, c. 2010.

from Taiwan, ready to strike at the 'rogue province' with ballistic missiles and artillery at a moment's notice.

Of concern not only to Taiwan but the West as a whole, is China's complete transformation of its war machine. The quashing of the famous Tiananmen Square protests in 1989 involved the PLA using its tanks and APCs to retake Beijing's streets with raw firepower. Today, a vast domestic security apparatus is in place for clamping down on any dissent. This freed up the PLA and its branches—the air force, navy, and rocket forces who control the nuclear arsenal—to use ballooning expenditures on new capabilities. These are the fruits of a defence budget that topped $144 billion by 2016.

In 2017, China launched the completed hull of its first domestically built aircraft carrier, the 55,000-ton Type 001A *Shandong*, while another state-owned shipyard launched the biggest warship in East Asia, the Type 055 guided-missile destroyer (NATO code name Renhai).

In 2017, the People's Liberation Army Air Force (PLAAF) received the first Chengdu J-20, a fifth-generation, multirole stealth fighter, a year after the introduction of the Xi'an Y-20 'Chubby Girl' military transport aircraft.

The People's Liberation Army, with its numbers trimmed down and reorganized under Xi Jinping, have new tanks, infantry fighting vehicles, artillery, and multiple-rocket launchers at its disposal, as well as the deadly effective ATF-10 anti-tank missile carrier, equipped with Hongjian HJ-10 missiles.

China's state-owned military-industrial firms are leaders in drone production and precision ordnance. The technology for microsatellites, offensive cyberwarfare, and stealth-detecting radars are within their grasp.

When it could, China acted like any great power, aggrandizing territory and trying to reorganize global affairs for its benefit. This hasn't stopped and, to cite a very specific example, in 2017 China did little to thwart its tiny neighbour, North Korea, from advancing its nuclear weapons programme.

Meanwhile, across the Himalaya, China acted the provocateur. In mid-2017, a standoff ensued in a remote borderland where China's, Bhutan's and India's frontiers intertwine. The PLA attempted constructing a road that would cut through the Bhutanese border. This activity was halted by Indian soldiers, but not without a brawl that was caught on video. The resulting diplomatic spat lasted the better part of two months and set back relations between New Delhi and Beijing, who are nominal allies in the BRICS association. Memories of the month-long 1962 war over Arunachal Pradesh stalked Indian newspapers for weeks on end, while fiery condemnation echoed from Chinese media. While the clash known as the Doklam Standoff was defused by a withdrawal of Chinese and Indian troops from the area in mid-September, the rivalry between China and India now appears permanent. It doesn't help that Xi and his counterpart Narendra Modi are both avowed nationalists whose political careers are built on the promise of leading their nations to greatness.

Xi himself is adjusting his image from a benign autocrat to what may best be described as a 'paramount leader'—a chief executive with direct control over the government's most vital tasks. This marks a departure from the governing styles of his predecessors, and is more in keeping with the late Deng Xiaoping.

This new guise was apparent on 30 July 2017, when Xi visited a remote PLA base in Inner Mongolia, a sparsely populated province known for its empty steppes and nomadic pastoralists. While in Zhurihe, Xi presided over an immense military parade dressed in his own battle-dress uniform. The ensuing spectacle made similar events in Russia, North and South Korea, and even Japan appear quaint by comparison. Having saluted the arrayed troops from the back of a car, Xi ascended a podium just as Changhe Z-8 (Zhishengji-8) multi-role helicopters—Chinese copies of the French Super

PLA Type-96 tank crews at the Shenyang training base in China, March 2007.

Frelon—swept down and disembarked troops in a mock assault. Another flight of helicopters flew past, forming the number '90'. It was auspicious, representing ninety years since the PLA's first battle in August 1927, also known as the Nanchang Uprising.

The parade itself involved dozens of vehicles that comprise the PLA ground force's arsenal, from self-propelled howitzers to all-terrain vehicles and nuclear-tipped ballistic missiles. Later on, refuelling tankers, early warning and control aircraft, and the PLAAF's latest J-20 stealth fighters soared overhead. The entire ceremony was broadcast on Chinese media and shared across government news outlets.

Most remarkable was the presence of Xi. This wasn't like the annual parades in Tiananmen Square, when the troops marched past Chairman Mao's portrait that gazes upon the distant mausoleum where his embalmed remains are interred. But in Zhurihe, Xi maintained his familiar stoic mien while delivering an address that hammered home why China's war machine mattered: "Today, we are closer

DF-5B 'Dongfeng' intercontinental ballistic missiles during a military parade commemorating the 70th anniversary of Japan's surrender during the Second World War, Tiananmen Gate, Beijing, September 2015. (Photo VOA)

to the goal of the great rejuvenation of the Chinese nation more than any other point in history," he said. These remarks are significant, for Xi expressed an idea that has echoed in Chinese thought and politics since the 1911 Revolution. But for Xi, 'rejuvenation' was just the beginning. In a speech that was filled with praise for the military, whose founders established the People's Republic, Xi reminded the troops of their reason for being: "The world is not all at peace, and peace must be safeguarded," Xi declared. 'Always listen to and follow the Party's orders, and march to wherever the Party points to!"

To which the assembled troops replied, "Follow the Party! Fight to win! Forge exemplary conducts!"

Mao Zedong defeated the Kuomintang and gave the Chinese people their independence. Deng Xiaoping dramatically thrust China's economy onto the global stage to become the world's richest country by GDP (IMF 2017 statistics). It is,

New Soviet Aid for Chinese

Yenan: Frank declarations of policy were made to me [special correspondent Edgar Snow] in this war-racked citadel of Chinese Communism by General Mao Tse-tung. Mao is the acknowledged leader of all the Chinese, Manchurian and Inner Mongolian Communists. He directs 500,000 troops, which operate from the suburbs of Shanghai to the Amur River—mostly in the rear of Japan's armies. And he sprung a number of surprises.

First, he denied flatly that the Chinese Communists had ever submitted to the Kuomintang (China's single official party, headed by General Chiang Kai-shek). The Communists were said to have accepted its leadership in 1937, when they joined up with Chiang as the war began. The Communist Party programme, Mao said, was completely independent of the Kuomintang and aimed ultimately at social revolution.

Next Mao talked of help from Russia, which he said was increasing as British and French aid was being withdrawn. But as a condition for increased Soviet military help in the future, he said, "China must unwaveringly continue the war against Japan and establish a closer political association with the U.S.S.R."

Finally, asked whether Soviet troops would invade Manchuria and Mongolia to aid the victims of aggression (as in Poland), Mao replied: "It is quite within the possibilities of Leninism."

Mao expressed his full support of Soviet policy in Europe.

"It is a logical part of the world liberation and revolutionary movement."

Daily Herald, Saturday, 21 October 1939

however, Xi Jinping who has converted communist China into the world's third strongest military after the United States and Russia.

Mao once said: "Let us imagine how many people would die if war breaks out. There are 2.7 billion people in the world, and a third could be lost. If it is a little higher, it could be half ... I say that if the worst came to the worst and one-half dies, there will still be one-half left, but imperialism would be razed to the ground and the whole world would become socialist. After a few years there would be 2.7 billion people again."

PLA guard of honour, 2012.

One of several Long March memorials. (Photo Zhangzhugang)

ABOUT THE AUTHOR

Born in Southern Rhodesia, now Zimbabwe, historian and author Gerry van Tonder came to Britain in 1999. Specializing in military history, Gerry has authored *Rhodesian Combined Forces Roll of Honour 1966–1981*; *Book of Remembrance: Rhodesia Native Regiment and Rhodesian African Rifles*; *North of the Red Line* (on the South African border war), and the co-authored definitive *Rhodesia Regiment 1899–1981*. Gerry presented a copy of the latter to the regiment's former colonel-in-chief, Her Majesty the Queen. Gerry writes extensively for several Pen & Sword military history series including 'Cold War 1945–1991', 'Military Legacy' (focusing on the heritage of British cities), 'Echoes of the Blitz', 'Death Squads' (on massacres and genocides) and 'Architects of Terror'.